The Communist and the Communist's Daughter

>+<

A Memoir

JANE LAZARRE

DUKE UNIVERSITY PRESS

DURHAM AND LONDON   2017

© 2017 Duke University Press
All rights reserved
Printed in the United States of America on acid-free paper ∞
Designed by Heather Hensley
Typeset in Garamond Premier Pro by Copperline Books

Library of Congress Cataloging-in-Publication Data
Names: Lazarre, Jane, author.
Title: The communist and the communist's daughter :
a memoir / Jane Lazarre.
Description: Durham : Duke University Press, 2017. |
Includes bibliographical references and index.
Description based on print version record and CIP data provided
by publisher; resource not viewed.
Identifiers: LCCN 2017010998 (print) |
LCCN 2017014623 (ebook)
ISBN 9780822372387 (ebook)
ISBN 9780822369370 (hardcover : alk. paper)
Subjects: LCSH: Lazarre, William, approximately 1903–1971. |
Communists—United States—Biography. | Lazarre, Jane.
Classification: LCC HX84.L35 (ebook) | LCC HX84.L35 L39 2017
(print) | DDC 335.4092/273 [B]—dc23
LC record available at https://lccn.loc.gov/2017010998

Cover art: Bill in Madrid, Spain during the Brunete Offensive, 1937.
Frontis: Bill, Kishinev, ca. 1915.

TO Ruth Sidney Charney and
Douglas Hughes White

AND FOR THE
CHILDREN AND
GRANDCHILDREN OF
BILL LAZARRE:

Emily Lazarre
Adam Lazarre-White
Khary Lazarre-White
Sarah Lazarre-Bloom
Simon Lazarre-Bloom
Aiyana Grace Taylor White

Members of the American Brigade, Spain, 1937.

Contents

Author's Note

Documents and references to works researched and read appear throughout these chapters. As I did not want to interrupt the flow of the story with footnotes or explanatory notes of any kind, all sources are cited at the end of the book. In general, I adhered to usage and spelling used in documents, for example, the lowercase *negro*. Bold sans-serif text is used for official transcriptions.

My father's name is spelled in various ways on various documents—Lazarowitz, Lazarovitz, Lazarowich—I have used Lazarovitz, as that is most common on legal documents.

The story of my father's sister Rose, some aspects of the portrait of my mother, as well as the re-creation of my father's thoughts, in italics, are combinations of traces of memory enhanced by imagination.

Front row (l to r), Bill, Uncle Buck; back row,
Tullah (on the right) and her sisters; 1940s.

Acknowledgments

I owe many kinds of acknowledgment in the writing of a memoir like this one. Friends, family, scholars, and writers I do and do not know all added to my learning and appreciation of the chapters of my father's life.

As I mention within the book itself, I obtained many of the documented materials of my father's life through the essential and dedicated help of Tom Manoff. I am filled with respect, gratitude, and ongoing affection for him.

A crucial find—the entire transcript of William Lazar's Appeal to the Court of Pennsylvania—was made by Jeremi Duru, professor of law and dear friend. I thank him for his help in many ways. For advice on research and a crucial introduction to the Archives of the Abraham Lincoln Brigade at the Tamiment Library at New York University, I thank Robert Sink, archivist and friend, as well as for always reminding me of the importance of preserving records of all kinds.

I am ever grateful to Peggy Belanoff for her expertise with computers and for always being available to help with the technological demands of this work.

Now I come to some people for whom words will hardly suffice to express my debt and thanks. For reading and for listening to the book, from the very early scenes to the last drafts, my writing group has stood by this work and by me, commenting, encouraging, and helping me to persevere through a long illness. Beverly Gologorsky, Jan Clausen, and Jocelyn Lieu—you are midwives to this work in every way—are wonderful writers, gifted listeners, superb responders, and dear friends. I owe a special debt to Beverly Gologorsky, whose generosity seems limitless, and who provided one of my first edits, giving me essential and perfect advice in her reading of the manuscript.

My dear friend and sister writer, Ruth Charney, read emailed chapters, listened to scenes, provided insights into our shared history, and edited complete versions over years of writing. My husband, Douglas White, and my son Khary Lazarre-White helped me with early readings, attentive response, and research; Khary's editing was always precise and incisive, and he was always willing to take over technology demands when computer anxiety had its way with me. My son Adam Lazarre-White, a gifted writer himself, read and commented on the book in its first completed draft. His knowledge of the difficulties in any artist's path strengthens me.

Miryam Sivan, Nancy Barnes, and Carole Rosenthal, all writers I trust and admire, read and responded to the almost final draft, giving welcomed suggestions, as well as confirmation and faith in the entire project. Leona Ruggiero, beloved friend and always a crucial reader, and Claire Potter, historian and lover of memoir, gave important support, each at a moment when I turned to them with specific needs. They and others—Joanne Frye and Lynda Schor—have helped to keep me going at various times during the years of this writing.

Phyllis Beren, Sarah Stemp, Josephine Wright, and Gary Schlesinger have worked with me on their writing for years, and are now both colleagues and friends. They read selected portions of this work, and discussed the forms of memoir and story and the poetry of language with me in ways that have taught me much as I listened and responded to their growing bodies of work—including discussions of the importance and difficulties of publishing in this time.

Which leads me to the unique person of Miriam Angress, associate editor at Duke University Press. She shepherded this book through its path toward acceptance at Duke, and was always uncommonly attentive, imaginative, helpful at every stage, and patient with my many questions and concerns. Her personal responses to this work have been a gift, and in this current publishing atmosphere, where many writers are so often treated with dismissals and disrespect, her work with me has been a true blessing. I thank her as well as Stephen A. Cohn, director of the Press, and all of the excellent workers at Duke who have provided copyediting, marketing advice and direction, and wonderful cover designs, and have performed many other tasks over many books and years. I am especially grateful to Sara Leone, project editor, whose knowledge, skill, and sensitivity to my work I cannot exaggerate. My great thanks.

I thank Adam Hochschild for his help through his own illuminating book, *Spain in Our Hearts*, and for his personal communications regarding directions for and corrections of historical material.

Although they are referenced numerous times in the book itself, I want to emphasize how much I learned from Peter N. Carroll and George Charney. Their books educated and inspired me throughout. I learned, too, from Edwin Rolfe's memoir and poetry, from Danny Duncan Collum's and Victor A. Berch's *African Americans in the Spanish Civil War: "This Ain't Ethiopia, But It'll Do,"* and from rereading George Orwell's classic work *Homage to Catalonia*.

No book or work of art stands alone. Consciously and unconsciously, we all build on what was written before. I am continually inspired and influenced by memoirs read and reread over many years, especially *The Woman Warrior*, by Maxine Hong Kingston; *I Could Tell You Stores*, by Patricia Hampl; *A Tale of Love and Darkness,* by Amos Oz; *The Pure Element of Time*, by Haim Be'Er; *A Sketch of The Past*, by Virginia Woolf; *Notes of A Native Son*, by James Baldwin; and *Patterns of Childhood*, by Christa Wolf. These writers set the standard for the genre of memoir—respectful of literary traditions yet revolutionary in creating new possibilities. I keep learning from them all.

My sister, Emily Lazarre, and my brother-in-law, Emanuel Bloom, helped me with crucial materials about the Spanish Civil War, including the history of the monument to the Lincoln Vets in San Francisco. I was so proud of my sister for her work on this project, especially when our family gathered at the monument to view it for the first time, surrounded by friends and families of the Abraham Lincoln Brigade.

My cousin, Miriam Goldberg, corresponded with me regularly as we tried to remember and gather information about our family history, and expressed a faith in me and in this work that meant very much to me.

I thank Jocelyn Lieu, Karen Flores Reininger, Daniel Ross, and Lisa Rodriguez Ross for their review and corrections of my Spanish.

Two people died before this book was completed, but both affected my life and work in many ways. My friend Sara Ruddick provided deep knowledge of the complex layers of family life in her writing and in our years of shared stories. Dr. Louis Lauro's wisdom and understanding enabled me to come to a new understanding of my father's and my story that gave rise to the original desire to write this book. I can't imagine this work having been written without him and the years of our work together.

Finally, one last time I want to thank my family. My sons, Adam Lazarre-White and Khary Lazarre-White, whose lives and commitments are a tribute to their grandfather, fill me with pride and gratitude. Their support of my work since they were old enough to understand it is an incomparable joy. My husband, Douglas Hughes White, lived through every stage with me, showing his usual patience, love, generosity, and faith in me. Without him, nothing, including my writing, would be the same.

Bill and his two sisters, Kishinev, ca. 1915.

Bill in the Party Office, ca. late 1930s or early 1940s.

Bill with his grandson, Adam, 1969.

It used to be all just a fog of thought, an intimation. There is a lot to be said for this writing things down. The fog gets pushed away, and the truth or some semblance of it stands stark and naked, not always a comfortable matter, no. But that was the task at hand, I suppose, to try my utmost to throw a makeshift bridge towards the future even though the iron work and the cables fade away to nothing in the distant air.

SEBASTIAN BARRY, *THE TEMPORARY GENTLEMAN*

... the fragments join in me with their own music.

MURIEL RUKEYSER, *THE POEM AS MASK*

Prologue

Therefore, the crucial distinction for me is not the difference
between fact and fiction, but the difference between fact and
truth . . . my single gravest responsibility is to tell the truth.

TONI MORRISON, "THE SITE OF MEMORY"

My father was a Communist Party organizer, a fervent believer in the political philosophy of Marxism-Leninism, the intellectual foundation of what
became a faith, ideas that had nurtured and inspired him since his adolescence in "the old country" of Kishinev, Romania.

Or Russia—he would always add—Russia, Romania—borders changing
with passing years and alterations in power, shifting national identities reflecting, it seems to me, other shifting borders and changes moving through
my father's life.

My father, a man with at least three names: his first, in the old country,
Itzrael Lazarovitz; the one on his citizenship papers, anglicized by himself, William Lazar, later to become Lazarre, an elegant addition of letters
made by his elegant wife, our mother; and his Communist Party name, Bill
Lawrence.

I use all his names in this memoir, a story pieced together from chaotic
shards of experience, memories both lucid and vague, at times consecutive
and coherent, then suddenly crossing time and space as sounds and silence
gather into images and words.

My father, Bill: a revolutionary leader, a commissar in the Spanish Civil War, and a teacher—labors with overlaps in methods and aims. He taught in a public square, and one of his early speeches there landed him in a Philadelphia prison in the 1920s. By the early 1930s he was teaching Marxism in the old Communist Party school on 12th Street in Manhattan. In 1931, the Communist Party sent him to study at the Lenin School in the Soviet Union. When he returned, he assumed a full-time post as a section leader to new Communist recruits and seasoned organizers. By the early 1950s, when his world and position had changed radically, he taught groups of Party members who were sitting around our living room to discuss current events and evaluate the swiftly changing politics of the time. And—always—through books, "discussions" and lectures at times—he taught his daughters, nephews and nieces, or any other Communist Children who were around and interested. He had been a writer too—of articles and essays about political ideals and strategies, and about the fight against fascism in the Spanish Civil War. My life as a writer and a teacher are in part a legacy from him. Through all the years, I have heard my father's voice, asking questions, expressing conviction, searching for the best words as he tried to explain.

"My blood is coursing through your veins!" he would shout at us, his children, when he was insisting on his love, or when he was angry, usually at me, for some rebellion too far from his principles to abide. I feel his blood coursing through my veins now—material genes, palpable and energizing.

Beginning this story, I hear his voice reminding me that no one escapes the forces of history in shaping ourselves. As my own education continued over years and I became a teacher myself, I wanted my students to come to see how our individual voices and silences are mirrored in the broader history of voice and silence. As I begin to write my father's story, I witness my sons, in different professional contexts also teachers, with the same questions and principles driving their work and growth. Blood seems to be coursing still.

I must have taken this knowledge in first with our childhood Sunday dinners—the broiled lamb chops and inevitable boiled chicken taking second place to dinner table talk about inequality, especially the inequalities of class—though he did not use that word with us when we were young. Working people, he would say—including Negro (the proper word then) workers, and women workers ("The Woman Question" always included in serious political talk)—were *our people*, the ones whose lives and interests we were never to move far from in our concerns.

But I was not always an ardent follower of my father's views and examples. Perhaps even more than the typical adolescent, I rebelled against him and some of his beliefs. In high school, where I majored in painting and sculpture in what was then the High School of Music and Art, I encountered ideas that reflected what I had always felt yet could not fully express—the complex realities beneath conscious perception and manifest appearance. In college I became friends with a group of English majors and poets who were already immersed in Freud's theory of the unconscious, how it applied to our intimate lives, illuminated the literature we were reading and planning to write ourselves some day. To use Toni Morrison's perfect phrase, I fell in love with the "deep story," and at the age of eighteen I began a long, traditional psychoanalysis. I was encountering a possibility of internal freedom not, in my mind, antithetical to my father's, and one of our long-standing battles began.

⊁⊀

Recently, I was standing on the shore of a peaceful bay at the tip of Long Island where on a clear day you can see the land across miles of water—the trees, the hills, a lighthouse, a boat approaching. Color and shape change dramatically with the angle of the sun. In a certain remarkable light that suffuses that stretch of beach as evening approaches, pinks and golds stripe the sky, lending striking triangular streams of glitter to the water that look like, though they are not, starlight. Both panoramas—the clarity of the first, the lit-up creation of the second—are equally necessary, equally real.

As I think about that view across the bay, the need for realistic perspective and also for lit-up imagination, I wonder about what Christa Wolf once called "the shape of conscience." Violence spreads across the Earth. Iraqis, Syrians, Nigerians, African Americans, and Latino Americans in our own cities, Americans of all backgrounds, including young children, are murdered, made homeless, incarcerated, suffering unbearable loss by the thousands. A few miles uptown from where I sit writing, my son directs an organization in Harlem that serves children and youth[1]—academically, emotionally, ethically, and legally—children who, if not for independently created organizations like this one, would be largely forgotten by a society of incomparable wealth, power, and possibility. My thoughts turn again to my father, the Communist, of his concept of human freedom, whose sources and contours for him were always social and economic, but a concept that without an imagined ideal would quickly have died.

His passion was for the world and its people. From his earliest years in the old country of his birth, he lived to increase justice, human equality, *dignity*—he would have called it. He risked his life and reputation to this end. But his most immediate and, it turned out, most compelling passion, especially after his wife died, was for the children—his two girls.

About a year ago, in dreams and unbidden fantasies, I was repeatedly crossing a bridge that reached across a river as wide as the Hudson that flows only a few blocks from my home. In my dreams about this bridge, coming toward me from the other side, sometimes vague in a cloud of mist, sometimes as clear as the city on a cold and bright winter afternoon, is my father.

I enter into his story as if into unknown territory, even though, unlike my mother who died when I was seven, I knew him long enough to really know him—even given the long years of idealization and anger we all retain for our parents, those easily blamed and eagerly criticized souls. I knew him in ways I never got to know her: I know his stories, or enough of them to have a good sense of his history over nearly seventy years, to be able to guess with at least some confidence how to fill in the blanks. I knew his power of language and analysis, the depression that stalked him on and off for years, his love of stories and of books, how nervous and anxious he could suddenly become. On Sunday nights, he would come into our room, sit on one of our beds, and begin a tap-tap-tapping motion with his fingers on a nearby surface, one of many motions signaling his anxiety. One of us named this feeling "the creeps." "I have the creeps," he'd say—and we'd all smile in recognition. We had no idea, then, he was anticipating a futile weekly job search that lasted for years after his leadership position in the Communist Party came to an end.

Every morning out he went, dressed in a pressed suit, always navy blue, a tie, blue-and-red-striped or a patterned blue and gray, fitted neatly beneath a freshly washed and ironed shirt, usually pale blue but sometimes white, and going—where? We did not know for years and did not ask. He must have walked the city, stopped in for a sandwich, gone to the library. Perhaps—I hope—he visited an old comrade in a similar position, lost without the Party, unemployable and untrained.

"What should I have put on my resume when they ask for employment history?" he'd ask us later when we were old enough to understand. "For the past several decades I've been working as a section organizer and high-level officer of the American Communist Party? And as for education? Finished fifth grade in Kishinev, Russia."

➺

Now that I have passed the age of sixty-eight, the age he was when he died, I know there is no certain blessing of absolute confidence in one's own memory or point of view. But at times and in some ways there can be a feeling of solidity and clarity, like standing in an old familiar place and thinking, *Yes. I know what happened here; I know who he or she is. Or was.* Or even, *I know who I am, who I have been, and who I have become.* Becoming a grandmother, being the daughter of a Russian Jewish immigrant and a Communist, being the white mother of two black sons and the wife of an African American man for over forty-five years—all these have shaped my consciousness and my conscience.

Yet only recently have I come to appreciate the depth of my similarities to my father, the virtues and faults I share with him, the very ones I used in fervent differentiation. (*At least I am not like that! I would never do that to my child!*) And I also know the opposite truth—how different I am from him, how different one can be even from those closest and most loved—a husband of nearly fifty years, two men who were once my own boys.

How different I am from my father.

How like him I finally see I am.

➺

As I began this work I wondered, How close to the bone dare I write? What shall I try to remember? What old notebooks do I retrieve from their high dusty shelf and reread? What is the scope of this search, this research—how to shape a blend of imagination, recorded history, and personal memory? What shall I make up? What does that childhood phrase even mean? How to capture in words the tones of a man long dead yet whose voice in my head is as clear at times as the actual voice of my husband, or a friend I may talk to every day. A man whose words could range from what now sounds like predigested rhetoric but was then a revolutionary vocabulary defining an ideology that promised to rescue the world; to the most naked cries of unmasked pain spat out into sound to the lyrics of songs in English, Russian, and Yiddish, memorized perfectly because they so perfectly fit his often overflowing emotions, to shouts of disdainful criticism; to a laughter so complete it generated liquefying spills from eyes and skin and mouth, all quickly wiped with a white cotton handkerchief grabbed out of a pocket, crushed into his fist for compulsive twisting and untwisting as he spoke; to frequent declarations of love for us, his daughters, the sacrifices he made for us backing up his passionate words.

My father: it might be possible to scale his-my-our story down to a clean boneline if his bones were not dust, cremated long ago, buried by me in the earth of my mother's and his brother's graves, which lie side by side in a huge, somewhat overwhelming cemetery in Long Island, New York, both graves overgrown and neglected for many years.

"Forgiveness,"[2] I called the story of that makeshift, long ago burial, and I believe I did forgive him, then newly dead and I, just twenty-eight with a two-year-old son to adore and a new husband to love. Everything seemed possible. Why not forgiveness? And forgetting. That too.

Now I am thinking of him daily again, the father I loved and admired, the father I raged against, whose judgments I railed against, one of the men — my life is filled with such beloved, powerful, endearing, at times intimidating men — who influenced me in immutable ways.

But it is not only my aging, of course. For many years he's been back and forth, out of sight and mind, then suddenly shouting and lecturing again, whispering love, singing old Russian lullabies and union songs, igniting my nightmares and my dreams: he's been alive all these years, huddled in an abandoned empty room, and I have neglected him, forgotten him, wreaking punishment, managing escape; or he is weeping those old prolific Russian tears, sobbing into his large, strong, heavy-knuckled, pale, beautiful hands; or he is smiling tolerantly at me after a battle about my current boyfriend, or a principle of political reality I have failed to grasp, the warmth and unashamed vulnerability of his being revealed as he pulls me to him, calling me "Baby," or *Ketseleh*, and we are both disarmed of our indignation and righteousness. He mumbles something in Yiddish or Russian. I can hear him laugh.

Not long ago I Googled him.

Imagine if he read this line. He'd think his crazy daughter had finally gone truly mad—he who died before telephone answering machines, television remotes, cell phones, computers of all kinds with their mysterious, industrious engines. Yet there he was, in Wikipedia, leading a strike in Baltimore with his old pal Joe Carlson.

So the voice comes. For now.

PART I *Beginnings*

Memoirists . . . do not really want to "tell a story." They want
to tell it *all*—the all of personal experience, of consciousness
itself. That includes a story, but also the whole expanding universe of sensation and thought that flows beyond the confines
of narrative and proves every life to be not only an isolated
story line but a bit of the cosmos, spinning and streaming into
the great ungraspable pattern of existence. Memoirists wish to
tell their minds, not their story. . . .

I could tell you stories—if only stories could tell what I
have in me to tell.

PATRICIA HAMPL, "I COULD TELL YOU STORIES"

CHAPTER 1

In the beginning there was being a child of American Communists, learning how to tell FBI agents who came to the door that Daddy wasn't home—in some cases it was ok to lie; shouting to other children in elementary school that workers of the world would unite, street cleaners were as dignified as doctors, that Negroes were the same as our white selves and deserved equality—and the ordinary American children screamed that we should go back to Russia.

><

In the beginning, overshadowing even our politics, which were our faith, our *life,* there was being a motherless daughter at the age of seven, and the daughter of an adored but at times severely depressed father, his life from 1949 to 1951 shattered by losses from which in some ways he would never recover.

><

In the beginning, there was a sense of being Jewish in old world Yiddish culture. One beginning in a world of beginnings, and therefore, first, a story of beginnings. Middles and endings too, of course, but later. For now, beginnings seem to dominate, even to devour.

><

It is 2014. I am seventy years old, one year older, or possibly two, as old-country birthdays were never exact, than my father ever got to be. It is March, but it feels like January—frigid, the sidewalks lined with piles and hills of iced hard snow, so getting out of my husband's car down in Battery Park City, then helping my ninety-year-old mother-in-law out of the back seat, is a challenge to balance. We are here to visit the Museum of Jewish Heritage, for myself because in one beginning of the story of my father and myself was a sense of being Jewish—however fiercely secular, Jewish to our very bones, immersed in a culture loud with the sounds and emotional tones of Yiddish—a language I never learned, except for the many phrases and single words that still somehow feel like my mother tongue, though it was my father's tongue, not my American-born, non-Yiddish-speaking mother's.

My African American husband, after being married to a Jewish woman and living within a Jewish family for over forty-eight years, is a sort of Jew himself, or sort of Jewish—having co-led Seders, lit Hanukkah candles, attended countless bat and bar mitzvahs, and in general claims a deep love—sometimes exceeding my own—for aspects of secular Jewish family life and its rituals. Still, for him this trip to the museum on a cold Sunday with yet another snowstorm predicted for late afternoon is a gracious act of generosity, common to him. He accompanies me here so I can feel this soil of my heritage, so that I can complete the writing of this book, a task which to my surprise and due to many factors turns out to feel far more dangerous, sometimes insurmountable, than I had imagined when I first got the impulse and idea. And for his mother—my mother-in-law and close friend—the trip fills a need simply to get out of the house during a freezing cold winter when her miraculous energy and famous mental acuity begin to fade.

So we embark—out of the car, into the larger-than-I-expected museum. By the time we exit, we have walked through only one exhibit—"Jewish Life a Century Ago: 1880–1930." Due to fatigue but also perhaps to deeper and more disturbing resistances, we have not seen the floor that recounts the Holocaust years, nor the years of reparation, post–World War Two.

In any case, it is the floor dedicated to Yiddish culture—photos, old films, an interesting juxtaposition of voices addressing the major Jewish perspectives on the future of the Jews—alternating philosophies summarizing Orthodoxy, Zionism, Socialism, Liberalism—all ideas that affected my father's life and therefore my own—it is this floor that compels me. The exhibits return my thoughts and feelings to a childhood in which Yiddish phrases, foods, attitudes, and humor dominated my life, sometimes in our own kitchen and living room, especially after our mother's early death, and even more so during our weekend trips to Philadelphia, where my father's old world sisters and their families continued to live since their emigration from Kishinev, then capital of Bessarabia, a province of Russia, now in the twenty-first century Chisinău, capital of the independent nation of Moldova.

And it is Kishinev, the sound of the word, vivid from my father's memories, images rising and falling, that weaves into my own imagination—that word, *Kishinev*. I hear it in the sound of his voice, in his tones and accents: *Kishinev*, something like the sound of Tevye singing "Anatevka," a melodic prayer, a gathering of images, limning and illuminating the longing and love for home. Born in or about July 1902 and so a small child during the infamous pogroms of 1903 and 1905, he must have grown up listening to neighbors and friends talking of horrific experiences and persistent fears, beginning to make plans to emigrate, to escape the increasingly violent anti-Semitism of their world. He must have heard the stories of murder, dismemberment, rape, eventually seeing his own elder siblings leave to make new lives in new worlds. When my father took us to that remarkable play, *Fiddler on the Roof*, feelings, memory, and knowledge must have joined in his mind. He wept and laughed until the waters of his infamously easy perspiration flowed, and he had to pull out the ubiquitous white handkerchief to wipe his eyes and blot his cheeks.

My sister and I had been taught how to iron these handkerchiefs for him by Rose, the woman who took care of us after our mother died—first the square itself, then fold into long thirds, iron the creases, then fold in thirds again, iron the creases again, and make a neat pile for his drawer, the one on the side of the huge mahogany desk that once held my mother's accessories— flowered handkerchiefs, artificial violets and small pink roses—to decorate her tailored professional wardrobe, the dark sleek suits, elegant dresses, and long fur coats she wore to her position as an "important buyer in the handbag department of Macy's," a job that supported the family when my father was a full-time functionary for the Communist Party. Most likely that drawer held other things too, but more than sixty years have erased some memories and I don't recall what else was kept in those special depths that somehow retained their mystery even though I looked into them many times. I do remember my father's laughter and tears when Tevye left Anatevka, families pulling old carts filled with everything that could be carried or packed, his soft cries of oy, oy, oy, and other words too, I am sure, also forgotten by me now, yet the name—*Kishinev*—never forgotten, one of the places I have never seen that feels like home to me.

✦

In the Museum of Jewish Heritage, among the many old films providing a soft gray light to the darkened galleries is one of five old women standing in a row, singing. They are probably younger than I am now, but they are heavier, and poorer, their heads covered with patterned kerchiefs, their feet in those old black oxfords with laces and heels, their cloth coats not quite covering the dresses whose hems hang low over thick calves covered in the kind of sturdy tan cotton stockings my grandmother used to wear. And what are they singing? It is a song I know in the deepest crevices of my brain, the oldest layers of my psyche, one I have not thought about in many years: *Tumbalalaika*, they sing, words whose meanings are as unknown to me as to my husband or mother-in-law, words repeated over and over again:

> Tumbala tumbala tumbalalaika
> tumbala tumbala tumbalalaika
> tumbalalaika shpiel balalaika
> tumbalalaika freylach zol zayn.

Soon after this, we decide to leave, all of us hungry and not eager to view the devastations to come on the floor of the Holocaust—not out of timidity or a desire for historical amnesia; we are all three avid readers and witnesses, even participants in history, including many parts that involve unbelievable cruelties, what my father would have called Man's Inhumanity to Man. We are simply ordinarily tired, ready for coffee and a piece of something to eat, so we stop at the cafeteria. It is oddly empty, and there is not much available food. But we buy chips and coffee, and sit by a large window with a view of the Statue of Liberty visible in the gray and misty harbor. The Latino or South American server disappears, and in a few minutes a white woman customer shouts to my husband, "Are you serving here?"—despite the fact that he is sitting at a table with others, his winter coat around his shoulders. He looks away, and so does she, and then we find our way back to the car.

><

Later that night, much later, when we have turned off the lights and I think I am sinking into welcomed sleep, all the words of the verses of "Tumbal-alaika" suddenly come to me so audibly it is as if someone is singing them out loud, and before I know it I realize I am wide awake and the someone singing is me.

> Shteyt a bocher shteyt un tracht,
> tracht un tracht a gantze nacht,
> vemen tsu nemin un nit far shemen,
> vemin tsu nemin un nit far shemen

And after I sing the chorus again, more comes—

> Meydl, meydl, ch'vel bay dir fregen,
> vos kan vaksn, vaksn on regn,
> vos kon brenen un nit oyfhern,
> vos kon benkn, veynen on treren.

The chorus again, and then I repeat the whole song, amazed and delighted by this sudden surfacing of words, a language I do not understand, and will learn the meaning of what I sing only the next day when I look up the translation on the Internet; a song of love—*What can grow without rain?*—of heartbreak—*What can cry without tears? Play the music on the balalaika.* Yet in the night I feel strangely as if I am singing in my first language—the music and sounds of words I seem to know in some way even better than the language of English I love, the content of my life's work and a fundamental ground of my identity. Still, there I am in bed singing in Yiddish and feeling, yes, this is me. And then I am silent while another thought fills my mind, which I thought was growing nicely dim, or at least vague, ready for sleep. I am listing places, again out loud.

"What are you doing?" my husband asks. "Places," I say, thinking these are the names of the places that make up the stories and myths of my life, the places that will shape this sometimes elusive book about my father—his life, his voice, his places like his words crossing over into my own.

The Jewish Heritage Museum

Ellis Island

Kishinev

30 Greenwich Avenue, New York City

Strawberry Mansion on the North side of Philadelphia

The Eastern State Penitentiary in Philadelphia, Pennsylvania, where he served part of a two- to four-year sentence under the Sedition Act for "attempting to overthrow the government of the State of Pennsylvania."

Barcelona, Albacete, the Pyrenees Mountains he climbed on foot. Spain in the 1930s, the battle against Franco's fascists, Madrid, where in 2013 I would travel, trying to imagine the lovely streets and wide boulevards filled with sounds of gunshot and screams like the streets and neighborhoods of Syria and Afghanistan and Iraq are now.

The SS *Kroonland* he and his parents and sister took from either Belgium or Cherbourg to New York.

The courthouse on Foley Square, New York City, where he refused to name the names the Un-American Committee (as we called it) of the United States House of Representatives wanted from him and others.

The vast nation of Russia, then the Soviet Union, vastly unknown to me, familiar and always home to him.

And places in books,

in documents,

in letters,

and in my own imagination as I try to find words to describe sounds, colors and shapes, experiences and history, all of which requires much more courage and effort than it would if I had only asked the right questions, listened to extended answers and ruminations when he was still alive. Sometimes, I hear his voice, his sentences—perhaps actual memory, perhaps created by some need or desire of my own:

I loved my mama. She dressed me like a girl for my first five years. I had long curls. Maybe until I was five. It was the old country way. Boys kept looking like girls until they were ready to be separated from their mothers. I have no idea why, but I am sure my daughter would have a theory, if not a diagnosis.

In the old country, baby, some people were rich and some people were poor, some were Jews and some were Christians, but nobody was neurotic.

Both in response to my involvement, from the time I was eighteen, with psychoanalysis, a theory and practice my father disdained. But my mother's colleagues from Macy's—where she had what we might now call a "straight job" accompanying her increasing work through her husband for the Communist Party, but a job she considered her primary career as well as a way to offset my father's Party salary (a figure somehow recalled so specifically!) of twenty-five dollars a week—these executives, her bosses, had left my sister and me each a legacy: five hundred dollars a year for four years, which was meant to put us through college. I went to City College, then free to anyone living in New York City, and used my money for four turbulent, healing years on a psychoanalytic couch, a decision my father was respectful enough not to interfere with despite his obvious disapproval. So Freud joined Marx in my educational upbringing, neither loved or studied with as much passion by me as the British and American poets and novelists I was reading in school, and yet my sense of who I was, who I am, though I am neither a revolutionary activist nor a psychoanalyst, is still entwined with both those iconic thinkers, just as my head is filled with the sounds and music of Yiddish words and phrases I do not fully understand.

CHAPTER 2

After many years of oceans and lagoons, rivers flow in my dreams. Oceans seem infinite, vast water worlds of changing tides, shallow and then deep again, calm and then wild. The ocean floor is filled with life, and it is dark. Like the unconscious, it seems unknowable except with special suits, glasses, dangerous unless you are tied to ropes to return you to the surface. Rivers are navigable. Across rivers, there are bridges, overpasses and underpasses, the beautiful walking bridges across the Seine in Paris, the large bridges over the Hudson and East Rivers of New York.

As I recall my river dreams, I sit in a neighborhood café, writing in a beautiful, old-fashioned leather-bound journal given to me by my son Adam on my seventieth birthday, and I am remembering "as if it were yesterday" clear words in my head—silent to everyone but me—instructions to myself on the day I learned of my mother's death. I was seven years old in 1951. It is one of my most vivid memories, never erased or modified until now, always available, like a piece of music in a recording kept in the disc player, frequently played. All I have to do is press a button, flick a switch, and there it is, the loud sound of my own voice inside my head, silent to the world, the mind of a child giving herself instructions now that reality has forever been changed.

I am stunned, although I have known for nearly a year that she would die, even as my father, my aunt, my grandmother, and our housekeeper who was also a nurse to my mother as she slowly diminished in her large white bed to a skeletal almost nothingness—even as they all lied to me, or told me in a whisper-shout, to be silent, never to say those words—*She is going to die*—not even as a question—*Is she going to die?* I watched her die, and I knew she was dying, and when she died I was stunned, as one is when someone close to you dies no matter how long you have known it was coming, even as you began to want it to come to end their pointless incurable suffering as well as your own. The stunned feeling, I think, comes from the vision of the final alteration, the reality we all soften and translate even after we have been close to death, close to the dead bodies of those we love, up as close as you can be. There is the final reality of it. The body is there, but the person is gone. It is obvious, and clear, and undeniable. If the spirit or soul is somewhere else, as you hope, if the beloved voice remains in your mind, the spirit or soul or voice is certainly not where it has always been, in the familiar beloved flesh. That body, literally left behind, is something else. It is an end, impossible to comprehend, and it is also a beginning.

I see myself standing in our large kitchen, walking into the adjoining living room through the square archway, over to one of the two windows that look out onto Greenwich Avenue, filling in a picture to go along with the words.

"Now you must make your daddy love you."

Those are the words in my mind, then and now, and they are coming from someplace unknown yet already familiar, as if I am hearing someone else talk to me at the same time as they are said in my own voice. So it must have been before she died that I developed this lifelong habit of a split voice, though for years I believed that my voice split that day, when she died and all the months of adult denials went up in smoke, like the very end of a long-burning candle, and I knew maybe for the first time that my thoughts and perceptions, though often denied by those I trusted and loved, were sometimes an accurate reflection of what I observed or sensed in the world around me. That was part of the shock too—that despite the denials of all the adults I depended on, I had been right, my feelings had been true, and this left me alone and lonely in a way I don't think any child can tolerate without finding a way to turn that sense of aloneness and abandonment into something else.

I turned it into images and words. My mother drew faces and scenes, a skill and an appreciation she taught to my sister and me, and she loved interiors—decorated our home with colors and patterns I see as clearly as I do the patterns and colors I love in my own rooms.

My father was always reading, books of history, fiction, political theory, poetry. My father loved words.

Now I wonder again about those words in my head and about memory itself: how it can suddenly open like stage curtains and reveal experiences, vague and shifting feelings sometimes hidden for decades, suddenly present again as one approaches old age.

My mother-in-law has an extensive reel of memory of her early years, details and atmosphere, even dialogue spinning in her mind as if she were writing the novel she surely would have written if the world, the American South and American race history in particular, had been one of justice and fairness, filled with the equal opportunities of the fantasy America, so different from what it was and is. The details of her childhood, early marriage, the community of black families living in Mitchell Wooten Houses, a project built for black families in Kinston, North Carolina, where my husband, Lois's second son, grew up—their life finds its way into many conversations and experiences over the years. Even Yiddish culture in Europe in the late 1930s sparked her own memories that day in the Jewish Museum—the long skirts she remembered her aunts wearing, an old manually worked black Singer sewing machine like the one her mother used to make their clothes. From the early 1930s to the late 1960s, when she migrated north following her children to New York, the details of her childhood, youth and young womanhood remain vivid and powerful, even as she forgets her keys, her whole purse, how many times she has called me about a date or a time or a phone number she needs, all manner of daily events.

✦

This slide into the story of my husband's mother is a not an accidental tangent. In my life, marriage into an African American family was another new beginning. Lois knew my father for two years before he died in 1971, when their first shared grandchild was two years old. They both loved him and took turns taking care of him during the day when my husband and I were both in school or working. And they loved each other, Bill, the aging Communist, debonair and courtly in an old world way, his speech laced with the Russian Yiddish accents of his nineteen years in the old country, and Lois, the still youthful, magnetic black woman of the American South. Frederick, her husband and my father-in-law, died young at fifty, when we, in the promising and naïve moment of just turning thirty, thought he was old. Their stories are so intertwined with my history I cannot speak of one without the other. Often when I return to my father's story, my husband's family story breaks in, changing and defining it in unexpected ways.

My understanding of American racism and African American history, in my family and in this nation, began with my marriage in 1968 to change the way I view the American Communists who were my childhood extended family. It altered my view of my father, and it changed him, too—the Kishinev-born grandfather of a black grandson, father-in-law to a black man who in his twenties joined the Great Migration as it began to reach its end; friend of a black woman whose grandmother had been a slave in North Carolina, with whom for two short years he shared a first grandchild, and with whom, though he would not know of it, he would share one more.

Experience changes and reveals but can also distort and petrify memory. My memory of my words to myself about having to find a way to "get" my father's love—*Now you must make your daddy love you*—has always been emblematic for me. But in the past few years, rereading some of his old letters, studying his history in the Communist Party and his involvement in the Spanish Civil War, writing poems and stories about him, exploring the latent intricacies of fantasy and dream, revising and reinterpreting my story in a long psychoanalysis—all have altered my understanding of those internal words I have seemed to recall with such searing precision. Of the reality of the words I whispered to myself I have no doubt, but my understanding of the reason for my feeling has changed.

⊁⊰

While he lived, my father affected my feelings and thinking through the books he gave me, the ideas he never tired of expanding upon, through the depression he was always battling—singing of it in songs of loss in English, Russian, and Yiddish as he paced the large kitchen, the central room in our apartment, back and forth, back and forth, his pleasant voice growing low when his back was turned and loud again as he came near the doorway to our room, thinking, perhaps, that we, his young daughters, were asleep, or instead, since he needed love and comfort as much as anyone I have ever known, hoping we were not.

I remember one night getting up out of bed and sneaking behind him, pacing while he paced. My hands clasped behind my back as his were, I gazed at his large bony knuckles, trying to keep time to his singing, trying to match my smaller strides to his larger ones. Above all, I hated to remain in my bed in the dark, hopelessly, helplessly, listening to him weep and sing.

In the years since my father's death, he has continued to change me and to affect us all—grown-up grandsons and a granddaughter, three of whom he never knew, as well as all members of our extended family, including my mother-in-law, who was no doubt surprised by the older white man who was so welcoming to his daughter's new in-laws, and obviously pleased by his open flirtations with her, as he openly flirted with all the good-looking women he ever met. Teasing her and Frederick, he would whisper loud enough for us all to hear, "Come on, Lois, let's leave old Freddie and run away together." Frederick would respond something like, "You ain't running away with anyone or I'll be coming after you with a gun"—all said with a chuckle, slowly growing used to this unlikely friendship with an older white man—and we all, including my father, would laugh. Only now, years later, do I wonder if he was trying not to think about the history of white men appropriating black women forcibly from black partners, husbands or lovers, or if my father—so clearly a foreigner, so clearly a friend—could really get away with the joke whose historical meaning he was either ignorant of or chose to ignore. The story told and retold still pleases her, and when she laughs I hear the musical rhythms of the black South mixing with that old Russian accent echoing in my mind.

*

I possess an old plant that has somehow survived for more than fifty years. It belonged to my father, given to him by his last wife, and when he died I brought it uptown from his Greenwich Village apartment to mine on the Upper West Side. It used to flower—two gorgeous pink lilies every year, usually in the spring. But for many years, as its leaves have thinned and browned, there have been no flowers, and only in the heat of the summer, when I move it to my narrow terrace which gets a strong morning sun despite the high risers now circling our building, does it with magical life force flourish again. No flowers, but wide dark green leaves grow out of the old pot, and they multiply until the scrawny stalks of winter have become a thick tiny forest. This year, when the morning frost began, I brought it inside as I always do, hoping its weakening leaves would survive another winter. By early November the long green stalks were thinning and browning again, draping wearily over the sides of the ancient copper soup pot that belonged to my mother's mother, preserved from her mother's journey from the old country of Russia to New York, now containing the plant that has grown old with me. And then, in early December, there were the familiar tight buds again, pink leaves barely but clearly visible through the cloak of green. I watched and watered and even whispered encouragement—for who knows with certainty what any form of life may include or exclude. The buds opened. During the winter when I began this writing the flowers bloomed. I am not so spiritual a being as to believe in this as a message or anything more than a mysterious climactic accident. But it is true that when my father died and I buried his ashes in the earth of my mother's grave, I merged some of them with handfuls of the dark soil that covered her bones, brought them home and buried it all again in the earth of this potted plant.

PART II *An American*

Besides,
They'll see how beautiful I am
And be ashamed—

I, too, am America.

LANGSTON HUGHES, "I, TOO, SING AMERICA"

CHAPTER 3

Old suitcases, the leather worn and scratched, others of thick patterned fabric, still others woven baskets, lids tied down by rope, a large old wooden trunk—all piled up chaotically—either left behind, their contents not passing inspection during the waves of European immigration in the early twentieth century, or donated much later by descendants of parents and grandparents who had carried them from old-country homes to ships that would take them across the Atlantic to America. Entering Ellis Island in the early years of the twenty-first century, I am impressed by the restorations: the original white tile floors preserved, their cracks and stains visible, dismal rooms where immigrants like my father and his parents and sister would have been questioned, given basic literacy tests, submitted to mental and physical medical examinations. All is left as it was then with no attempt at romantic distortion: a museum, not a testimonial.

In the wide hall where crowds must have waited their turns for admittance to the rooms where they would be subjected to various evaluations, hoping, most no doubt praying, for admission to a promised land, a red-tiled floor stretches beneath a huge domed ceiling. Benches of pale gray stone line the sides of the room for the few—I imagine—who were first in line and could sit as they waited while hours passed, sometimes days. Steerage passengers like Bill, then still Itzrael, his parents, and younger sister Sima, might already have waited for many days on the ships before the ferries to the island retrieved them for their turn to enter the immigration center; or perhaps they sat on these very benches, stood where I am standing now. A descendant but also a tourist among many others—I gaze into glass cases containing old photographs, worn prayer books, yellowed health cards, some of them marked "passed." "Everyone was terrified," reads one page of an opened diary translated from the original Russian on a printed card; "Men in uniforms. In Russia, we learned to be frightened of uniforms."

Again, I am aware of all the lost family stories, the sisters and brothers-in-law long dead, my living cousins having little or no information themselves. There is a Hearing Room, where relatives already in America can testify that the new immigrants will not become "public charges." Did Rose and Leza, or their husbands, Dave and Abe, come to vouch for the brother and sister, the parents who had left everything known for this new, promising exile? There is a gate at the end of the rooms of examinations named "the kissing gate." Here, new arrivals and relatives already settled in America can finally meet and touch. I imagine my grandmother, Sliva Lazarovitz, seeing her two eldest daughters for the first time in years—Raisela and Eleza—rushing to embrace them, to feel their bodies in her arms; or holding back, an exhausted and confused mother confronted by these young Americans, married women, here to take her to someplace called Philadelphia. How much if anything at all did she and their much older father know of their sons' involvement in revolutionary politics, a commitment that both of them would keep in different ways until their own deaths? One is right here under their noses, only nineteen, his blond hair grown long on the long voyage, having led them from Kishinev to the trains crossing Europe and finally to a faraway place where they would board the huge ship that was to take them to this new unpredictable life, his obligations as a son overriding his own desire—despite the Cossacks, the pogroms, the anti-Semitism all around them—to remain at home. The other son God knew where, traveling toward them perhaps even now, or maybe lost or dead years before. Itzrael and Itzaac, soon to be William and Isaac, then Bill and Buck.

Buck would show up suddenly months later, his journey from Kishinev to "the East" then somehow across Canada and south to America never described to the family—there is no story to be carried down, only vague myth with absent detail: *Uncle Buck went East from Kishinev, came across the Earth all the way to Canada, traveled down to Philadelphia.* By then, Bill would have a job in a textile factory where he earned a meager living to contribute to the household of his brother-in-law David, owner of a small jewelry store in the front of his and my aunt's home in Strawberry Mansion, then a Jewish neighborhood in North Philadelphia.

><

"North Philadelphia!" I hear the conductor shouting our stop on the train as we ride south from New York City. My father, my sister, and I have come to Pennsylvania Station early in the morning to make the always-exciting trip to our relatives on our father's side. Our mother has recently died, and my sister and I sit on our suitcases as instructed by our father while he goes to the window to buy tickets. We stay absolutely still as he directed, excited by the crowds, probably also a bit frightened, holding hands. On the train, we are enchanted and relieved by seats that can be turned to face each other, so we can all be together, neither of us separated from our father, who is our Rock of Gibraltar, our tree of life, no matter his depressions, the sorrowful songs that fill our apartment each night. Our mother is dead. In our minds and with our hands we cling to him.

In Philadelphia, I will sleep in a high bed given over to me by my beauti-ful eighteen-year-old cousin Shirley, who is soon to be married. I will sleep under her soft quilt, made by my Uncle Leon, as we are allowed to call him, though everyone else calls him Llyova. It is the early 1950s, and you can still hear a rooster crow in the morning. I will feel luxurious and strange, com-forted by my old-country Yiddish-speaking aunts, who argue about who will feed their brother first, who makes the best food they pile in enormous bowls and platters on their cloth covered tables for us all. "Eat! Eat!" they will insist, even as we take more and more onto our flowered china plates. After all the food is consumed, or as much as I can eat of the rich kugel, sweet *tzimmis*, dark soft pot roast (for my father the forbidden pigs' knuck-les, sisters disobeying ancient food laws to please the brother who learned to love pork in prison), I will listen to my cousin Miriam tell me stories about going to rock-and-roll concerts—she once heard Frank Sinatra in person!—and she actually wears the bobby socks that have given her gen-eration a name.

It is a strange land for me, completely different from the Manhattan apartments of my mother's sister and the other Communist families with whom I am so familiar. American-born or long-standing Americans, most of them are college-educated, businessmen, even businesswomen, as my mother was, teachers, artists, even lawyers—but all of them Communists—some in leading positions in The Party, a name I have already learned to see and hear in capital letters. This is my world—the world of the Communist families, the near-kin community in which outside of school I live my life. It is a community I love, where I am loved as "Bill's daughter," where my father is a revered leader, where during the day and sometimes at night meetings I overhear him teaching and discussing while I am trying not to fall into my nightmare-filled sleep, recurring dreams of loss and desperation. But on other nights I hear him weeping. When I run into his bed, crying out that I want my mother, often finding my sister already curled up next to him, I fall asleep listening to his heavy sighs.

Here in Philadelphia my father is happy. He teases his sisters, annoying them on purpose, clearly delighted as he condemns their father for his brutality toward them all, especially his sons. *Papa is dead,* they whisper-shout, looking over at us, *let him rest in peace.* He switches to Yiddish, including a few English phrases—*no father to me*—dismissing their criticisms as they turn back to the stove, shushing him, dismissing him with their hands, trying to silence the conflict my father clearly enjoys. He welcomes visitors who come into the house especially because they know he is there, old men from the old country, some of them orthodox Jews dressed in long black coats and broad-brimmed hats I have otherwise seen only in photographs. These men with their full beards embrace my father, and he embraces them, laughs, talks with food in his mouth, reminiscing, I suppose—a feeling of being home, I somehow wordlessly understand. For the whole weekend, he is not depressed. So I too feel at home.

➤←

Was it the Yiddish language, I wondered—though I did not then have words for my wondering—that opened the door to his passing happiness as his sorrowful songs sung to us before sleep, also in Yiddish, gave lyrics to his despair?

One night, to my regret, I had asked for a translation:

You ask me my friend, how old am I? I tell you I do not know.
If living means sorrow, then I have lived so long; I've lived for many a year.
But if living means sharing the slightest bit of joy, then I wasn't yet born.

He says "borrun"—with heavily rolled r's. "It's 'born,' Daddy," I murmur wearily, hoping for sleep, turning my back to him, "not borrun." I roll my r's even more heavily than his, angry, yet also teasing him, trying to get him to laugh. Secretly I believe he is purposely exaggerating his accent, because I have heard his English, I know his capacity for beautiful phrasing and articulate rhetoric on many subjects, the voice of a deep alto tenor, words pronounced oddly at times but always perfectly chosen. I am fascinated by and attracted to his voice.

Years later, when I begin to write his story, to read the documents of his trial in Philadelphia in 1928, at which he will be accused and convicted of sedition, and even later his brilliant, sardonic, yet unfailingly principled testimony before HUAC in 1958, when I begin to imagine his first sighting of the Statue of Liberty in New York Harbor, it is his facility and devotion to language that will fill my mind and my page.

After nearly a lifetime, still determined to find an indisputable connection to him.

1921

The SS Kroonland *has arrived in New York Harbor after weeks at sea. The famous imposing green statue stands where he has always seen her stand, in postcards, in pictures. He cannot read the words, not in English, not yet, though he already has a careful plan to study as soon as he arrives in Philadelphia. Hoping his brother-in-law will meet them on the mainland, he almost prays to the old god in whom he has long since stopped believing. He crowds onto the deck with the others, the "huddled masses"—among the few words and meanings he knows, the English letters engraved somewhere on the base on which she stands, the phrase engraved in his memory. His father has put on his thick glasses, trying to see as much as possible. His mother's eyes, red-rimmed from crying, might be mistaken for eyes filled with infection by examining officials, and he tries to quell his anxiety, always an accompaniment to his courage and determination, always nearby, threatening to drag him down. He and his sister are fine. Nothing at all wrong he could find in his own meticulous inspection that morning. And yes, he tells himself, his mother's eyes are clearly red only from tears. He turns his thoughts from fear to hope. His sister Raisela has told him in a letter that within walking distance of her home there is a public library, open to all, even to Jews. There he will be allowed to borrow books to learn English, maybe even an evening course if he can find one for free.*

Over the past months he has learned the English alphabet, ever since it became clear he'd have no choice—he would have to go—bring the others, leave comrades and meetings he loved, his dreams, all his plans. He had never finished primary school, but his mind was good. He learned fast from the books he devoured whenever possible, books describing a better world, a revolutionary movement sweeping the land. His learning is accelerated by his passion to understand, his understanding deepened by the clarity—the logic—of the lessons learned from pamphlets, newspapers, borrowed books. There was no one else. No one had heard from Itzaac. An older brother, Dovedal, had left so early for America Bill hardly knew him. Bubbe was old, would soon die. So in between the evening meetings and rallies, after long hours working in the old man's tearoom, sometimes in a stolen afternoon sitting in the hills looking down on the city he hated yet still loved with all his heart, he studied the alphabet in an old English dictionary he found in the shul.

He has memorized through t, was now practicing u, v, w (always confusing the two); x ("Ecks," he says out loud, practicing, glad it was rarely used); y or vy? (the problematic w again); and z, easiest of all.

As the ship moves slowly past the statue toward the island where they will disembark, he reads the words letter by letter, copies them into his small black notebook so that later, with Raisela's help (she calls herself Rose now—the name given to her when she arrived, an American Rose), he will be able to read them in English. As they were meant to be read.

"Keep, ancient lands, your storied pomp! Give me your tired, your poor, your huddled masses yearning to breathe free, The wretched refuse of your teeming shore. Send these, the homeless tempest-tossed to me. I lift my lamp beside the golden door."

Into the tiny notebook he has written the letters of the words that will inspire him through all the years, that will name his own relation to her—Mother of Exiles—and he will one day be able to say, "The wretched refuse of your teeming shore, send these, the tempest-tossed to me."

And to me, he silently adds, vowing lifelong commitment as he copies the letters of the words he knows only in the Russian translation. But one day he will read the poetry correctly, exactly as it is etched into the stone. He closes the notebook and shoves it deep into his pocket. He will learn English. He will master it. He will continue his work here, he will join the Party, but he will be an American.

CHAPTER 4

We all give credit to this man of learning. It is so very obvious, and it will be better for all concerned if he recognizes that fact and intelligently and directly answers the questions that are propounded to him. That is all we ask of him, but we are not going to turn this court into a public meeting for the purpose of elucidating theories and premises and principles.

JUDGE OF THE SUPERIOR COURT OF PENNSYLVANIA,
COMMONWEALTH V. ISRAEL LAZAR, APRIL 1929

It is April 1929, only a few months before the beginning of the "Great Depression," which would commence officially in October of that year. But to most Americans—workers increasingly unemployed, families evicted for lack of funds, and certainly to international Communists who study the waves and storms of capitalism with a close eye, judging its possible wreckage and the opportunities that wreck might open to radicals who wish, with no sense of arrogance, rather with idealism and hope common to revolutionary movements aiming to change the world—to all these the predictable catastrophe is already here.

Bill's mother and father are dead. He is by then an organizer for the American Communist Party but also off and on a knitter in a textile factory where he earns enough to pay rent and put food on the table for himself and his young wife, also a Communist, also an immigrant from Russia.

At about 8:15 on the evening of August 28, 1928, on the northeast corner of 13th and Reed in Philadelphia, he stood on a small wooden platform—a box really—and made a speech to about fifty people, the number reported by the police officer who arrested him; later Bill would claim the crowd was closer to one hundred. He had no way of knowing at the time who, if any, were sympathetic to him or to the Communist Party he represented. He was a young organizer, almost ten years in this country, already committed both to democracy and to a revolutionary concept of social change, liberation from the broad and deep injustices of capitalism that so many believed was about to fall into "the waste-bin of history."

How, he would often wonder in years to come, could any worker not see the benefits of socialism, a state serving those who created the very means of production that kept the nation wealthy and alive. But he understood the power of propaganda. Down through the centuries and all over the world people supported policies and leaders hostile and inimical to their own interests. As a revolutionary, it was his job to use all his powers, sacrifice everything if necessary, to attempt with words and deeds to penetrate ignorance and paralysis, to obey the leaders of the Party that would deliver a new world to the people, even if that obedience sometimes went against his own intuition or personal analysis. He—they—were engaged in a collective struggle, and leadership was a necessary part of the coming victory.

Yet someplace within him, the battle always waged—between his rational analysis and his belief. Call it naïve, he would say, even sentimental (he was a sentimental Russian, he would say proudly when criticized or mocked for the intense emotion he could rarely hide). He would rather call it passionate— a passionate belief in The People—the individuals he loved and the collective he lived to serve. He read and reread the essays and books until he knew his Marx and Lenin almost by heart. He understood in his soul (he still used the word soul) who was the oppressor, who the oppressed. And he was willing to sacrifice his liberty, even his life if necessary, to bring these ideals to fruition.

William Z. Foster was the Communist Party's candidate for president of the United States of America in 1928. He had no chance of victory, of course, but it was nevertheless imperative to run him, to use the opportunity to educate the masses—even if only a portion of them would listen at first—to begin the work of breaking down ideas cemented for centuries, to try to force open the locked doors of prejudice and ignorance.

The cop who arrested Bill—*for speaking*, he would insist at his trial—despite the so-called protections of the First and Fourteenth Amendments to the US Constitution—a Constitution he himself fully believed in—did not intimidate him. Prison was in the cards for a revolutionary, even desirable, and he had been arrested twice before—once the charges dismissed, once in jail for only a few nights. Now he had been found guilty by a jury of his so-called peers, as he supposed they were, and the appeal now in progress held only a remote chance of victory. As he sat at the defendant's table in the imposing courtroom, he probably repeated to himself that prison was an important experience for any revolutionary, a rite of passage. Still, responding to the appellate judge, answering his own lawyer's questions as well as those put to him by the Commonwealth of Pennsylvania in the repellant person of Theodore Rosen, assistant district attorney, he must have had to concentrate to contain his fears.

>+<

Over eighty years later I am reading the record of the *Superior Court of Pennsylvania v. Israel Lazar*, appellant, the father I knew long after his release. When his appeal is denied, as it will be, and jurisdiction for further appeal to the Supreme Court of the United States is denied a hearing, he is in his middle twenties. By the time I am born, in 1943, my father is about forty. Reading his responses to the interrogation by the DA, the insistent demands of the judge, the questions of his defense lawyers who try valiantly to give him the chance to explain his thinking with familiar finesse, I cannot always know if he is distorting the seditious words he is accused of speaking or if they have been distorted by his enemies. But when I read his words, when he speaks to the court on the pages before me, I can see him. I can hear his voice.

>+<

The arresting officer is quoted in the appeal, his testimony spoken at the time of the trial read to the court:

He said, "this government murdered Sacco and Vanzetti"; he said "This government is a strike-breaking government"; he said, "Let us teach our young workers in time of war to shoot down the people who ordered us to shoot on other people." Other workers—was the words he used. He said, "The only government in the world is the Russian Soviet." He said, "President Coolidge and Secretary of State Kellogg is a bunch of hypocrites."

. . . I warned him; when he said it a second time I said, "Cut it out." The third time I told him to get off the box. Then he said he had a right to give a speech; "I will have you arrested," I said. He says, "That is what I want you to do." I says, "All right, I will accommodate you." I arrested him, and that is all there was to it.

His only hopes were the very constitutional protections he had come to value, that he had sworn to uphold when he became a citizen. And he had meant what he had sworn. The contradictions—and he knew there were some—between these protections and the necessity at times to override them in the struggle to literally alter the direction of human history—were clear to him. These contradictions—argued and battled within his own Party right up to the present moment—were now about to land him in prison. He had no doubt of this. But this was not the time to ponder contradictions or attempt to see the future, however obvious it was becoming. He had to find some way of explaining to the judge what he meant by "revolution," the ideas he stood by, where he had been purposely and dangerously misunderstood.

He was asking people to vote for William Z. Foster on the Communist ticket?

His lawyer's question of the officer on the stand, to which the answer was yes—and he followed with other pertinent questions.

Did he mention that the Communists stood for the seven hour working day?

Did he say that the Communists would put into effect unemployment insurance?

Did you say there was any disorder?

The answer to that last question had been no.

At times, I suppose, the young defendant was surprised to be given the opportunity by the presiding judge to try to reiterate in his own words what he had said then.

I pointed out the fact that we live in the richest country in the world, he had been permitted to say. **That the amount of wealth of the United States exceeds**

four hundred billion dollars, and at the same time . . . as a matter of fact, a vast majority of the population does work and produce and those people, in spite of the tremendous wealth we have in this country, those people possess nothing but their labor power, and on many occasions they are subjected to misery and starvation.

He paused, thinking he would surely be interrupted, but he was allowed to continue.

I spoke about the fact that people in the South are being forced to work for ten or twelve dollars a week working fourteen hours and fifteen hours a day; that the men who are employed are in fear to lose their jobs because of the fact there are so many workers unemployed. I pointed out the fact that on many occasions when workers under the pressure of that miserable economic condition can no longer stand those conditions and they go out on strike against the bosses, they immediately face the police, they immediately face the militia, who always protect bosses against working men. I bring out how the negro workers in the South are being discriminated against, how lynchings are taking place—and I pointed out the fact that negro workers are always being mobilized to fight against the white workers that especially negro workers in the South are ones who work for low wages, are the ones who live in misery. I pointed out that the negro workers are disenfranchised and not allowed to vote on many occasions, and I also pointed out that our party, the Communist Party, which is a party of the working class, is the only political party in this country which raises the slogan of social equality for negro workers. I pointed out that the Communist Party was the only political party that raises the slogan of no race discrimination, and raises the slogan of equality for all races, all nationalities.

From the beginning of the appeal, the defense team made the argument that Bill's First Amendment rights were being denied due merely to a campaign speech.

Again and again the defendant attempted to clarify his intent, to elaborate his arguments and demonstrate that he had not been advocating the overthrow of the government by violence but to change the government by vote.

In the final appeal, rejected by the court, the argument reads, **The utmost** latitude of expression must be accorded to those who are seeking political change, whether moderate or extreme, through the ballot, and continues with reference to previous case law:

> When the admitted intent and primary purpose of the speaker is to get votes for his candidate, the fact that 'his ranting utterances had for their ultimate purpose the undermining of the stability, and the usurping of powers, by force, of the constituted authority' (quoting the prosecution here) is not enough to destroy the equal protection clause of the Fourteenth Amendment.

And later the legal argument for appeal, referring back to the arresting officer's testimony:

> This in effect is police censorship. . . . This man was arrested for calling the President a hypocrite . . . it is fair to say he was convicted for calling the President a hypocrite . . . given a severe sentence [two to four years] in part because he called the President a hypocrite. In practical effect a Sedition Act has been perverted into a law of lèse-majesté.[1]
>
> This is no less its practical effect because the Superior Court in sustaining the conviction quoted such words as 'revolution' and 'violence' which made so little impression on the police . . . that they could not remember that the defendant used them. . . . In this case, however, the direct and immediate purpose was to get votes; . . . The defendant, a radical, was arrested and convicted for doing exactly what radicals are told they must do—seek their political changes through the ballot. In such circumstances, it should be the function of the Courts not to determine whether enough can be squeezed from the more perfervid flights of his language 'to turn the color of legal litmus paper'; but rather to determine whether in fact he was engaged in an attempt, not merely to 'undermine the stability' of the government, but definitely to overthrow it by violence. A Statute that jails a man for anything less goes outside the legitimate field of a Sedition Act and infringes on the constitutional right of free speech.

The decision, as he had predicted, was upheld. Bill—Israel Lazar—was remanded to the Eastern State Penitentiary for two to four years.

But not before he sparred with the judge about the meaning of words, the complexities of revolutionary rhetoric, and the general conditions of working Americans. In the process of what I can only read as a debate between Bill and the judge about what we might now term "discourse," context, implication, and intent are argued and parsed with attention to specificity more common to academic meetings than to a trial. Reading the record so many years later, I am struck even more forcefully by the contemporary parallels. I admire my father's uncompromising insistence, combined with what must have been a hard-won patience in that young man, less than ten years an English speaker, only five or six years an American citizen. And I assume that however fully he had become accustomed to American life, images of the old country—its Cossacks and militia on the lookout for Jews, its infamous prisons—could not have been far from his mind.

Yet referring to the Kellogg Peace Pact that included millions of dollars for military appropriations, and despite continuing interruptions, he proceeded to reiterate the assertions of the speech that had gotten him arrested in the first place:

Yesterday, I stated a Peace pact was signed known as the Kellogg Peace Pact, and I pointed out—

The Court: Leave out what you pointed out.

Attorney for Lazar: Leave out the expression 'I pointed out.' Just say 'I said.'

Witness: All right.

The Judge then asks the witness to remember his words as he spoke them, not to elaborate, a request which will be repeated several times until the request becomes a demand.

Witness: I am trying to, Your Honor, but I am being interrupted every once in a while.

Once in a while. This phrase stops me. I recognize in my father's rhetoric this common use of satire, even mockery, both in political argument and in the personal conflicts between us during my childhood and adolescent years. We argued about my way of dressing, my temper, the hours I spent lying on my bed staring at the ceiling rather than doing something productive. We always made up though, a tight embrace, his wet kiss on my cheeks and forehead, the scratchy feel of his unshaven beard if it were a Sunday night, when, for some reason, our arguments seemed to escalate. I would go to bed relieved by the confirmation of his love but also still furious at him. Now I understand that criticism and mockery can be a defense, at times born of a desire to cause pain or to diminish, but at other times a sign of desperation to be heard when you know you are more likely to be ignored or misunderstood.

><

The court, unmoved by either sarcasm or desperation: **You need to be interrupted.**

So the witness proceeds, perhaps with a sigh of resignation, a swift touch of fingers, then tongue, to lips:

> **I stated the Peace Pact was not the means really to prevent war. The Peace Pact, I said, was merely a means in order to disillusion the people. . . . to make them believe we are really trying to eliminate war.**
>
> **. . . I said that as long as you live in a society which is based on profit and exploitation, which is based on the misery of others, war is inevitable, and I called upon the workers to vote for the Communist candidate as an expression of will to take that money which is being appropriated for military purposes to help the unemployed workers of this country. I called upon the workers, both white and colored—**
>
> **Q: What did you say when you called upon the workers?**
>
> **A: That is what I am going to state, Your Honor. I called upon the workers, both white and negro, to support the . . . party that is fighting for the white and negro workers, to support the party that stands for unemployment insurance, that does not want to see workers and children evicted from their houses because they have no money to pay the rent.**

Later in the cross-examination, his name and occupation are demanded.

Israel Lazar, he will say. When asked if he goes by any other name, contrary to what he will feel he has to insist upon years later during his testimony to the House Committee on UnAmerican Activities when McCarthyism rules the land, he will state for the record with no apparent hesitation, **I am known by the name of William Lawrence.** He then provides his current Philadelphia address, that he has lived in this city for nine years since arriving in America, that he is a textile worker by trade but is currently out of work.

From there, the Court begins its questioning regarding the use of the word "murder" in reference to the recent executions of the Italian-born Anarchists Sacco and Vanzetti, despite international outrage and building denunciations of the clear injustice of the sentence. This series of questions is central to both prosecution and defense. If the defendant stated that the government "murdered" the famous anarchists, that is cause for a verdict of guilty according to the interpretation of the Sedition Act under which he is being tried. If some other more precise word was used—"executed," for instance—the implication is that the defendant recognizes the legality, if not the justice, of the government's actions.

The Court: What did you say . . .?

And again, the judge insisting repeatedly on the verbatim words, not the "elaborations" the defendant clearly prefers, not what you spoke about.

A: I am trying to do that. . . . I said that the Government of the United States represents the bosses' classes and operates in the interests of the bosses.

Q: Did you or did you not say that the Government of the United States was responsible for the murder of Sacco and Vanzetti?

At first he acknowledges this and answers, I did. But a few interchanges later, perhaps warned by his attorney (the record does not include any interchange if it did occur) he amends, If I may correct you, if you will take it. I said that the Government was responsible for the execution of Sacco and Vanzetti.

The argument as to whether the word "murder" was used continues. The witness advises the Court that, there are quite a few errors in this testimony,—referring to testimony in the original trial, and finally states unequivocally for the record,

I used the word execution and not murder. . . . I said the Government was responsible for the execution of Sacco and Vanzetti.

The Court: And you say what I have read you [using the word "murder"] is incorrect?

A: Incorrect.

There are many more pages of testimony in which Bill's language is argued: Did he say workers should turn guns on their oppressors if there is another war?

A: What I stated—

Q: Just answer yes or no.

A: The way you put the question it is impossible for me to say yes or no.

He asks for the question to be repeated several times, perhaps an intentional delay so he can strategize. He tries to explain the Marxist view of war—no doubt aware of the futility of his effort but clearly wanting the idea to be recorded into official testimony—that wars are begun in order to obtain material profit for the ruling class.

This is during the aftermath of World War One. The war against Franco's fascists in Spain is some years away, and its closely following aftermath, the fight against the Nazis in World War Two, is more than a decade away. In 1928, this is a different world than the one in which Bill will live out his thirties, forties, and fifties. Even in 2015, the arguments taking place are hauntingly familiar: issues of racism (Black Lives Matter), inequality of wealth (Occupy Wall Street), and the then unimaginable powers now exercised by corporate America—all will be debated with increasing intensity with each subsequent twenty-first-century presidential election.

When a war breaks out, the young Communist is saying in 1928—a patient teacher, his students clearly ignorant of even the basics of historical forces: **When a war breaks out, it is not because I, let us say, or someone else hates a German or a Russian fellow, because as a matter of fact, we have never met together, but someone sent us to war we find today.**

He is cut off. Legal arguments ensue once again, regarding the defendant's alleged call upon workers to shoot their officers instead of their enemies.

No, the witness will insist. He would not and did not say such a thing.

Asked if he said that when the Communists get into power they will do away with those now in control of government:

A: Yes, I did. And what I meant was, that as soon as the working class of this country will get this government, or whoever they be in control of this Government, that we will eliminate from the Government bosses who do not work and do not represent the oppressed worker, the white and colored workers, as well as the poor farmers. . . . And I mean [he clarifies after a few more questions] **any government on earth.**

He tries to lecture the Court on Communist Party doctrine at a time when he still believes fully in that doctrine: that through education, organizing workers, and forming alliances, the working class will realize the government is using force and violence against *them.*

Finally—for there is no doubt the defendant used and uses the word "revolution," asserting that it is likely a revolution may be necessary—the meaning of the word becomes the center of the argument, and the defendant is allowed to explain his beliefs:

A revolution may be a result of an evolutionary process. A revolution must not necessarily be a bloody one.

I hear my father's most cautious, practiced voice, by his forties and fifties when I knew him well a distinctive sign of his style of debate and instruction, even when he knew he was sliding over complexities he would prefer not to allow into the discussion. Even in his twenties he must have sounded convincing and in a way appealing when he spoke that way—a quality of charismatic certainty difficult to resist.

And that is when the judge, asserting his right to determine the atmosphere and discourse of his court but including in his assertion either a compliment or a note of sarcastic insult, states,

We all give credit to this man as a man of learning. It is so very obvious, and it will be better for all concerned if he recognizes that fact and intelligently and directly answers the questions that are propounded to him. That is all we ask of him, but we are not going to turn this court into a public meeting for the purpose of elucidating theories and premises and principles.

Counsel for defense is then allowed to ask about his client's views concerning elections. Are they any use? Are they of little use?

A: It would be of little use, because we find today a very small percentage of the population participating in the election, that the negroes in the South are disenfranchised and are not allowed to vote.

There is a move to strike, but the Court asks: **How do you know that the negroes in the South are not permitted to vote?**

A: How do I know it?

Q: Yes, not hearsay, how do you know it?

A: It is an established fact.

Q: Wait a moment. How do you know that?

A: I happen to read the press every day. I happen to be acquainted with the events that take place in the South and not only are the negroes disenfranchised—

Q: Were you present at any of the elections in the South at which the negroes were not permitted to vote?

A: I was not.

And so the response is stricken from the record.

Q: (again for the defense): What did you say about carrying the message of the Communist Party Program to the people?

A: What I stated was that the Communist Party participated in the election campaign in order to bring forth the problems of the working class to the attention of the worker. The program of the Communist Party calls for education . . . and organization of the workers to fight for better conditions, lower hours of work, and higher wages, and we utilize the election campaign in order to educate the people and bring the problems of the working class to the attention of the workers.

This of course is before most American workers are organized into unions, before the labor movement begins to articulate similar goals and strategies, certainly long before unions become a powerful voice, a force for and at times against racial equality in the United States. Moreover, during this time, the "popular front" philosophy—that alliances between revolutionary and progressive forces are desirable and useful in the fight for social change—was the official position of the American Communist Party and of internationalist Communist doctrine, as well as of Bill personally, who was soon to be centrally involved in union organizing.

Later, the court returns once again to the issue of names.

Q: Can you give any reason why you use two names, Lawrence and Lazar?

A: I will.

Q: You can do it briefly.

A: I was once arrested under a charge that was at that time dismissed . . .

Q: Why did you have two names?

A: In order to save a job.

And later:

Q: Are you an American citizen?

A: Yes sir.

Q: Were you born in this country?

A: No, Sir.

Q: Are you naturalized?

I am holding the petition issued by the US Department of Labor's Immigration and Naturalization Service in my hands. It states that on April 1, 1927, a certificate of naturalization officially granting him citizenship was issued to Israel Lazarovitz. Ten years later, in 1937, Israel Lazarovitz will officially and legally become William Lazar. Some years after that, when he is newly married to his second wife, Tullah Deitz, my mother, she will add the other *r* and *e* to the name, making Lazarre the name by which both of their children and eventually their grandchildren will be known. Various stories have been told about my mother's choice to add the French-looking ending to her husband's already anglicized name. A sense of pretention reflected in her choice of traditional British-Protestant names—Emily and Jane—for her Jewish daughters? Or perhaps, in a more lighthearted mood, she was adding a touch of humor and her characteristic flair to her husband's fairly common Jewish name.

But in the doomed appeals, Israel Lazarovitz will still possess only two aliases: Israel Lazar and Bill Lawrence, the Party name he carried in many situations and circles for the rest of his life. Even at his funeral, some of the old comrades referred to him as Bill Lawrence, my sister and myself as Bill Lawrence's daughters.

Attorneys for the defense (including lawyers for the American Civil Liberties Union, or ACLU) continued to appeal, despite repeated refusals by ever more superior courts, that the speech made on the evening of August 28, at the corner of 13th Street and Reed in Philadelphia, was not a call to violent overthrow of the American government, therefore not **a clear abuse of the inestimable privilege of free speech and [was] inimical to public welfare,** and not punishable as an act of sedition. **Citizens have the right freely to express their opinion though it be unpopular and in criticism of the officials of the United States,** they will assert, and that any statements by the defendant were not in any case **so derogatory of the President of the United States and of the Secretary of State as to subject them to hatred and contempt.**

But the conviction of the lower court was upheld, the Supreme Court refused to hear the case, and William Lazar, alias Bill Lawrence, alias Israel Lazar, served a portion of the two- to four-year sentence.

In my father's FBI file obtained many years later, in many Internet searches, and in family lore, the shortening of the sentence is referred to both as a "pardon by the Governor of the State of Pennsylvania" and as an early obtained parole. In the story of the pardon, my father, clearly enjoying hiding secrets or concocting provocative tales, would insinuate that the daughter of the then sitting governor must have been in love with him. "In love with you? The daughter of the *governor*?" I would ask, loving the idea, begging for details. But my father would only smile his most enigmatic smile, click his tongue, and shift his eyes, refusing to elaborate. In the parole story, he would claim to have recruited two of his three parole officers into the Communist Party. In both stories, he obviously enjoyed our gasps of delight when we were young, our skeptical eye rolls when we were old enough to doubt and wonder. I would later learn that Governor Gifford Pinchot of Pennsylvania, a man of progressive leanings, may have recognized the severity of the sentence for what was, after all, only a speech. In an ACLU document, "Land of Pilgrim's Pride, 1932–1933," recalling the atmosphere of fear and legal disobedience to the American constitution during those years, it is stated,

"An important victory was the commutation of the two to four year sentence of Israel Lazar. He was released from Eastern Pennsylvania Penitentiary by action of the State Pardon Board and Governor Pinchot. He had served a little over a quarter of this minimum term." Elsewhere in the same document, the "pardon" is referred to as an early "parole."

≯≮

I like to remember all the stories, and I know that those months in prison affected him in many more ways than his late love of pigs' knuckles. He used the time to read as much of contemporary American fiction as he could, favoring writers such as Dreiser, Upton Sinclair, Sinclair Lewis, and others who were exposing the poverty and cruelties endemic to American capitalism, especially during what was, by then, the time of a full-blown depression. And his love of singing songs learned in each successive period of his life included one called "Springtime in the Rockies"—a song he said he had learned from a fellow prisoner with lyrics that described the loneliness of a long and painful separation. "When it's springtime in the Rockies," he would sing, "I'll be coming back to you. You will always be my sweetheart, with your bonny eyes so blue." Though my sister's eyes are blue like my father's, and mine are brown, I loved to hear him sing that song with its promise of reunion, no matter how delayed.

There were many moments even during the trial when Bill's love of stories and their many possible versions became contentious. When he says, "I then elaborated," the Court insists at one point, **That is something he says now to change what he said then.**

Bill's attorney, clearly knowing his client well, responds, **He uses that word. It sounds good, and he loves to use that word.**

The Court, uninterested in rhetoric, let alone poetry or stories responds, **Don't use the word and don't elaborate. Just say what you said.**

And so it goes, and went, to no avail despite all elaborations and explanations.

What seems undisputed is that for whatever legal, political, or romantic reason, Bill is released from prison after about eight months and moves to New York City, where he resumes organizing for the Party and begins to teach in the Communist Party school on 12th Street in Manhattan. There, among his other students and recruits, he will meet his second wife, my mother, her sister and brother-in-law, and his friend George Charney, who will become like an uncle to me, father of my oldest lifelong friend, Ruth. George's memoir, *A Long Journey*,[2] begins with an introduction by Michael Harrington asserting the universal and critical importance of socialist principles. The memoir narrates George's move from dedicated organizer to party leader and official, through his ultimate devastation after Khrushchev's acknowledgment of Stalin's murderous policies at the Twentieth Congress of the Communist Party, to his work to try to reform the Party. The effort fails—engendering further battles and splits. In 1958, along with two other prominent leaders, he resigns from the Party that has given his life meaning for many years, and to which he has sacrificed much, including a number of years in prison when his children, my sister and I, were very young.

During that time, I spent many nights with his daughter, Ruthie, both of us trying unsuccessfully to sleep in her narrow bed, listening to all the grown-ups in the living room discussing George's imprisonment and the need for bail. We would inch out through the small hallway and peer through the doorway, where we saw the grown-ups we relied on and revered, who took care of us all in a world that could sometimes be close to communal, all gathered around the long oak table counting a growing mountain of one, five, ten, and twenty dollar bills. We are using it to buy George back from jail, they told us in response to our fascinated questions, and we were sent back to bed.

I will read George's memoir many times in the course of writing this book, especially the many sections about his comrade, Bill Lawrence. During some of the worst Party splits, they would be on opposite sides, their long solid friendship broken for several years. Despite my father's unsympathetic response to the book when it was first published as too much of a compromise with American liberalism, much of its historical clarity and retrospective balance will help me to understand their illusions during years of denial of the tyrannies of Stalin and Stalinism, but also to appreciate anew the ideals of human equality and "a better world" they held so close to their hearts and minds.

The working class must own and profit from the means of production their labor creates. From each according to his ability, to each according to his need. This was the credo they passed on to us. It was the overriding value that many of us, the "red diaper babies," tried to continue to uphold at least in our personal lives, both at home and at work, even as skepticism of its possible implementation on a broad social and economic scale grew.

George would write of his long journey, "it is not easy to win from a man this conviction that our life had meaning."

From 1930 to 1958, Bill will devote himself to these ideals despite the doubts that periodically assail him. I have read various accounts in which he is described as a follower of Jay Lovestone, the Lovestonians, as they came to be called. Once leader of the American Communist Party, eventually expelled on orders of the Soviet Communist Party, Lovestone was philosophically a follower of Nikolai Bukharin who asserted that each national Party had a right to interpret Marx and Lenin according to its own history and conditions. A close associate and friend of Stalin's, Bukharin was eventually executed for his revisionist views. As I read and recognize some of my father's opinions, I seem to recall that at times his views were consistent with Lovestone's. In other memories, he is speaking of Lovestone and "the Lovestonians" with a tone of contempt. At first, wanting a clear and coherent story about the Party and Bill's place in it over four decades, I read and reread attributions and scenes as contradictory to each other as were the contradictions within the ranks of American Communists at the time. Finally I realize it is futile to try to ascertain *the truth*. This story will not fall into perfect coherence or singular clarity.

What I do know is that the arguments taking place throughout Communist Parties and governments were taking place within individuals as well, and Bill would swing for years between rigorous obedience to the idea of a "vanguard of the elite" and a more truly revolutionary spirit that questions, that refuses to see life in strict dichotomies of good and evil. Though he cannot deny the reality of evil, the fundamental goodness of human beings remains his most cherished belief. It is a contradiction he, along with many of the rest of us, will never resolve.

≫≪

In 1936, Francisco Franco's fascist army invades Barcelona and Madrid in a move to topple the elected Republican government of Spain. The United States and other western democracies refuse to support the Republican resistance in what becomes an increasingly brutal civil war. When Communist Parties, including the American Party, begin to send volunteers who will join the International Brigades fighting alongside the Spanish people, Bill will be among them. In early 1937, he will cross the Atlantic headed for the south of France. With other comrades, he will climb the Pyrenees Mountains protected by the dark as they make their way on foot, and once in Spain, he will travel to Albacete, where he will serve as base political commissar.

He will go as a Communist who believes above all in internationalism, who perhaps cannot imagine the mass genocides to come, the rise of national and ethnic hatreds, the brutal murders in the name of patriotism and religion the world will soon witness, continuing to the present day. He has always believed in what—for the present moment in 1936—the Soviet Party professes: that alliances between Communists and other liberal and progressive forces are crucial, that these alliances are the only means by which fascism will be defeated. Since boyhood under the belt of a tyrannical father, since adolescence as a Jew in anti-Semitic Russia, since arriving at Ellis Island and making his home in America, he has believed fervently in democracy. When he goes to Spain as a member of the Abraham Lincoln Battalion, later known as the Lincoln Brigade, he will go as a Communist and as an American.

He may not be thinking of his arrival decades before at Ellis Island, or about his first sighting of the Statue of Liberty. Certainly, he has no idea that someday he will have two daughters, four grandchildren, two of them African Americans, no longer called "Negroes" with either a capital or a small *n*. These two grandsons will be descended on their father's side from enslaved Africans and Civil Rights workers who, like himself, will spend time in American jails for exercising the rights of citizens, and on their mother's side from political activists and immigrants, Jews from Latvia and

Kishinev. Many years later, their mother and their maternal aunt, along with two sons-in-law he called "son," will have his name engraved on the American Immigrant Wall of Honor at Ellis Island, marking the place where more than seventy years earlier Itzrael Lazarowitz began his journey toward becoming William Lazarre.

If this war is to be forgotten, I ask in the name of all things sacred, what shall man remember?

FREDERICK DOUGLASS,
LIFE AND TIMES OF FREDERICK DOUGLASS

In October of 1937, "Bill Lawrence, the popular and hardworking American Political Commissar of the International Brigades base," left Spain after months of "unstinting and fruitful activity." In making his departure, Lawrence left the following message:

"I am sorry that I could not say goodbye in person to all of the men with whom I have had occasion to speak during many months we have been here together.... In leaving I have many things to say but you already know what they are ... so I will skip the speeches and make this farewell short and to the point.... We as one small part of the Peoples' Army, should be proud of this fact; we should be more than ever determined to continue the fight to its only logical conclusion—victory for democratic Spain."[1]

Introducing comrade Johnny Gates as the next political commissar, with many compliments and assurances of continued approaches to the work of defeating Franco and the fascists, he ended with the words "Carry on just as you have carried on, improving always, together with our British and Canadian comrades, as well as all our other nationalities in the International Brigades, and with our Spanish fellow fighters. Salud, comrades!"

Once back home, still working for the Spanish cause, and in early 1938 still hoping for victory, he wrote in *Democracy's Stake in Spain*, "The Communist Party of Spain starting from the premise that the main issue before the Spanish people is to win the war, realizing that unity is the prerequisite for victory over fascism, guides its work and formulated its policies continuously and consistently along the path of endeavor to unify all anti-fascist forces of Spain."[2] He recounts stories of individual soldiers, most of them involving heroic deaths, sacrificing themselves to save others; he extols the profound friendships formed between men who knew nothing of each other before Spain, and asserts the crucial role of the Americans in the battles of Jarama, Brunete, and Madrid.

"We must demand," he writes, "that America with its democratic traditions does not desert a bleeding nation, struggling for liberty and independence. We must intensify our efforts to draw the Socialist Party into a movement for Spain. . . . We must help deliver the death blow to world fascism."

During the years of the Spanish Civil War, through the following decade and especially during the Second World War against Hitler, Bill's faith and his analysis were in harmony, faith enhanced by the heroic efforts of the International Brigades, analysis confirmed by political views coming from Moscow. Politics and love aligned, his comrades were well known, his enemies clear, his position of leadership in the Party appreciated, by some even revered. His mind and his body were strong.

I know this from stories told to me by uncles, comrades, by himself—from reading histories and memoirs. I did not know my father during this period, when he was apparently at the height of his powers. When he returned from Spain, he married my mother, by all accounts (with the exception, perhaps, of one woman he loved during the last years of his life) the love of his life. It may have been a marriage of great difficulty. I heard repeated stories of a crucial affair of my mother's, one that almost ended her marriage to my father, but I have no way of knowing if this story is true as it was told to me by my mother's sister, her mother, and our housekeeper/substitute mother/caregiver, all of whom had reason to lie and frequently did so.

The sister, my aunt, did not trust my father in many ways—about money, feeling he had squandered what my mother left, and about how he was raising my sister and myself, especially me, whom she believed she understood far better than he ever could. She loved him, I think, but she loved him with a kind of patient disdain.

His mother-in-law, our maternal grandmother, who had lived with us all my life thus far, feared a new marriage would banish her from his home. After months (or perhaps it was years?) of provoking nighttime terrors in me with stories of impending Christian orphanages and cruel Jew-hating nuns if I did not fight any new marriage, I finally told someone who told him—and he did banish her, but only to her daughter's home, the aunt who had lived with a lifetime of anger at her mother, coupled with an adoration of my mother, an idealization I now believe served to hide jealousy of the "beautiful, brilliant, elegant" sister, favorite daughter of their mother's heart.

Our mother-substitute—"housekeeper/caregiver" (there are still no adequate names for such women whose love for the children in their care is often deep and familial, yet who are, in the end, paid and hired to replace absent mothers, their own lives and troubles most often hidden from us, their "adopted families," who often know little of them)—Rose had her own story, which she bled into mine, its metaphorical blood flowing as deeply as if she had used a sharp kitchen knife. Like herself, she said, my father was unknown, not Bill but the man with whom my mother had the supposed affair. She hinted at the mysterious origins of my birth but swore she would not tell me the whole truth until I was eighteen; when I reached that age and demanded the story, she told it. Years later, during a period of reconciliation and closeness to my father that was partly a result of my marriage and the birth of his grandson, I recounted that story to him. He became furious and called Rose to confront her. She had not worked for us for many years, but we had all remained in close touch. She denied it all, told him I had always been a liar and was telling lies now. She repeated this accusation more than once in the early years of my adulthood, when I still knew her and visited her, that I was a liar, and it's a strange one to me, as others have sometimes accused me of telling unwanted and unappreciated, sometimes hurtful truths. When she died, I did not attend her funeral, and when I think of it now, all these years later, I feel a mixture of remedy and regret.

But all this happened long after the Spanish Civil War and the world war that followed had come to an end.

CHAPTER 6

In 1969, when he was in his late sixties, Bill suffered a heart attack. The incident preceding it was the death of a woman he had come to love. She died of cancer, just as my mother had, only this woman, a late-life love, had moved far away from him after her diagnosis, not wanting him, she said, to experience the trauma of witnessing the dying up close for a second time. I traveled to a hospital in Philadelphia (he had been visiting his sisters) where he had been treated—not with surgery, at that time uncommon, but with various drugs. The serious-looking doctor asked me if my father had experienced any large disappointment of late, and I vaguely remembered the story of this woman, so my father must have begun to tell us about her. "I think a woman he was deeply involved with just died," I told the doctor. "That would do it," he said, smiling sympathetically, and advised me to take care of my father during his convalescence. In the last trimester of my first pregnancy, I attended graduate school in the city, and my husband, Douglas, about to enter his last year of law school, worked for a law firm in New York during the summer, so between the two of us we began to nurse my father back to health.

⇥⇤

My father's stories, always for him a primary way of connecting to others, and I believe an essential way of comprehending his own emotional life, came regularly that summer. And we listened, Douglas fascinated by a life very different from his own in many ways, and yet in other ways filled with parallels. A young man leaving home (the South; Eastern Europe) and moving to large cities of the United States (New York; Philadelphia). While trying to earn a living (setting up and taking down tables in a midtown hotel in Manhattan; weaving cloth in a factory in Philadelphia), the "real work" from adolescence on (civil rights demonstrations against enforced legal segregation in the South leading to tenant and community organizing in East Harlem; joining the Communists as a teenager in Kishinev and then, in adulthood, working to organize workers and recruit young radicals to fight for that better and more just world)—this primary work for both men—"soul work," I would call it now—continued.

I had heard some of the stories before, and some, responses to Douglas's eager, direct questions, were new to me. So I listened too, cool, damp washcloths draped on my body, most of the rooms lacking air conditioning during that hot New York summer. My advancing pregnancy increased my discomfort in the heat, and it was a relief to listen closely to my father's stories and his manner of telling them. Perhaps I even wrote them down someplace now long lost or misplaced in an old file or suitcase at the top of some closet, thinking that perhaps someday one of them would find a way into the books I hoped to write. But I have searched through closets and drawers, old files and fraying boxes, and what I have instead of records of his stories is the classic, regretful cry of the memoirist, whether in poetry or prose: *Why didn't I get it all down, save everything carefully, every spoken and written word?* Yet something remains. Old stories surface. Feelings long ossified by rigid beliefs suddenly emerge. New perspectives are slowly released by time, altered by experience and age, and sometimes even feelings change.

In his small bedroom at the front of the apartment that summer and the following one during my son's first year, it is neither the FBI nor the Party trials Douglas is most interested in, but war. The Vietnam War is raging, and though Douglas has an exemption, we are all shocked and enraged at our government, really unhinged by the immediacy of slaughter as, horrified, we watch the first televised battles not softened by the foggy gray of newsreels or historical film, not distanced into long past history, but war in its terrifying progress—faces of men the same age as we are being shot at, killed and killing before our eyes. Villages burning, mothers and fathers screaming, injured, maimed, crying or dead children in their arms.

Douglas has been intrigued since we met by Bill's history as an American radical, an actual Communist, and as a veteran of the Lincoln Brigade in Spain. My father has displayed his black béret, its Brigade insignia sewn tightly to the front, and his worn leather gun belt to his new son-in-law, as well as his collection of books personally and preciously inscribed, including a gold-leaf leather-covered set of collected papers and speeches of Abraham Lincoln, given as a special gift to every surviving Vet. No doubt memory was sparked, if memory of those days ever needed much sparking for Bill. He would recount stories of Spain often; he would write of Spain to his grandson long before Adam could read. He would leave us books about

Spain, invoke those years of hope and belief in letters and talk throughout his final years.

+←

From high shelves and old sealed boxes piled in the closest I have recovered various books I took home after my father's death, one especially compelling and new to me: *The Lincoln Battalion: The Story of the Americans Who Fought in Spain in the International Brigades*, by the poet Edwin Rolfe.

Madrid, 1936:

On Saturday, December 26, 1936, at three in the afternoon of a crisp and sunny midwinter day, the S.S. *Normandie* churned away from its dock in New York Harbor, bound for its home port at Le Havre. Very few travelers had booked first-class passage. The tourist cabins were half filled. Only the third-class quarters were unusually crowded for the holiday sailing. The number of passengers in this section was swelled by the presence of ninety-six young men, few of whom had ever before crossed the Atlantic. Most of them were in their early twenties. All were bound for Spain.

These men [the volunteers that made up the Lincoln Brigade] . . . were within a few days to face a crack army in one of the most sanguinary battles of modern history. They were to launch an attack over open, unprotected terrain against some of the best soldiers in the world—Franco's expert and ferocious Moors [mercenaries recruited from Morocco, to the south]—and to stop them.

. . . After two attacks under deadly enemy crossfire, only a hundred and fifty remained of the four hundred who had fired their five rounds against the Castilian hills.

. . . In the year and a half that followed, more than two thousand other young Americans followed the original volunteers into Spain. They came from every state in the union, climbing the perilous snow-covered Pyrenees in the darkness of night, crowding the holds of small fishing boats on the Mediterranean.[1]

Long after those years of struggle and hope, Bill's son-in-law persists, insisting on memories and stories, hoping for revelations, evening after evening as summer moves toward fall.

"What was it like in Spain?" he asks, respectful in his tone, long moments of silence somehow emphasizing his desire for specifics.

"Tell me something you were involved in that might not be in the public record."

A list of Franco's atrocities follows. The imprisoning, torturing, slaughtering of thousands—the centuries-long mad desire for "Spanish Catholic purity"—an extreme religious hatred that was soon to reach unimagined peaks in the war in Europe to come. Spanish soldiers loyal to the Republic, volunteers from Europe and America, captured and summarily executed.

"In 1937—February," he told us, recounting information I had heard many times before, the battle of Jarama. "First time in combat for the young boys—they were soldiers supposedly, but with hardly any training, and there were countless deaths." I see his face becoming slightly drawn, his posture more awkward—was he tapping the end table? I don't recall but he may well have been—and I remember some of what he told us next.

At some time during November of 1936, A. G. Mills (a false, perhaps Americanized name, I would later read—his real name being Sam Milgrom), a high functionary in the Party, called my father and Ed Bender, two of his "most valuable subordinates," to a meeting in New York. There had been a shift in policy toward the war in Spain, first from the Soviets, then from the American Party. Bender and my father, both known for their grassroots organizing skills, were charged with organizing and screening American volunteers to go to Spain. Travel by ship to France would be legal, but from there into Spain the men would have to find their own way over the Pyrenees. Ultimately, many of these recruits would die.[2]

The awkward movements in his chair, his face drawn—he must have been thinking of his own role in recruiting those young men, some passionate to defeat fascism, others merely looking for adventure, never imagining the horrors of actual war, many of whom would never return.

"We—they—fought like real heroes," he said. "I never lost my respect for them, or the picture of those young faces signing up in New York, never knowing what would hit them in the next year."

᳝

Now it is easy to find firsthand descriptions by scholars Bill would never know, one of them Peter N. Carroll, chair emeritus of the Abraham Lincoln

Brigade Archives (ALBA), professor at Stanford University, and author of *The Odyssey of the Abraham Lincoln Brigade: Americans in the Spanish Civil War*:

The Lincolns moved into new trenches on February 23 and then received orders to go over the top for the first time.... They numbered exactly 373, officers and troops. Backed by a pair of Soviet tanks that distracted enemy fire, they advanced through thickets of olive trees, firing sporadically at the fascist lines. They drew a light return fire—until one of the tanks billowed in flames and the other clambered away in retreat. Left exposed to rifles and machine guns, the Lincolns clawed for cover. Of the battalion's eight machine guns... *[one of the leaders]* reported, 'none was working.' Screams of 'first aid!' filled the air. But the slightest movements drew a hail of bullets and efforts to rescue the injured invariably multiplied the number of casualties. Stranded in the open fields at nightfall, the Americans stumbled back to their lines.... The day's toll: 20 killed, nearly 60 wounded.[3]

And from Helen Graham, professor of Spanish history at Royal Holloway, University of London, author of *The Spanish Civil War: A Very Short Introduction*: "Despite these desperate losses to the Americans, Republican forces, with Russian tank and air support, stem[med] the rebel offensive which threatened to cut the Madrid-Valencia highway."[4]

᪥

In July 1936, the military rebellion against the Republican government of Spain had begun. Within two weeks, Hitler and Mussolini decided to aid the rebels by sending planes to Morocco to airlift much of Franco's army to mainland Spain; in October, the International Brigades began to arrive; in November, the battle for Madrid was in full force, aided by bomber pilots sent by Hitler and Mussolini. The United States and England refused to help, enacting embargos and "gentlemen's agreements" with Italy. In April, the Vatican established relations with Franco, and one after another the liberal democracies of the West abandoned Spain.

Reading the history that in the twenty-first century is rarely taught or known, I remember the names of the Vets I knew or knew of: Steve Nelson, Eddie Bender, the paternal uncle of my first cousins, Ernest Arion, who died in the early days of the war, the photographs and names of those I read about or heard speak at annual reunions of the Veterans of the Abraham Lincoln

Brigade, their voices and memories strong in aging bodies, their numbers diminishing over the years. In the spring of 2008, my father long dead, I attend the opening ceremony for a monument in San Francisco to honor the Lincoln Brigade. Designed by Ann Chamberlain and Walter Hood, it is one of four tributes in the United States honoring those who fought in Spain—there are two other monuments, in Seattle and in Madison, Wisconsin, and a memorial plaque at the City College of New York commemorating thirteen volunteers, students, and professors who died in Spain.

※

North of the Harry Bridges Plaza at the Embarcadero, in sight of the waterfront of the Port of San Francisco, rises a long and broad structure made of stainless steel framing onyx panels containing the images and words of veterans and related events, visible on both sides. My sister, Emily Lazarre, an artist who lives in the Bay Area, worked for months on the committee to oversee the design and building of this testimonial, and now our whole family was gathered—spouses, friends, sons and daughters, our granddaughter seated on her father's shoulders as he told her the story she would be told repeatedly, as faithfully as the yearly story of Passover. Walking around the beautiful monument, I read the inscribed words of Paul Robeson: *The artist must take sides. He must elect to fight for freedom or slavery. I have made my choice. I had no alternative.*

And the famous cry of Dolores Ibárruri, called La Pasionaria by Republican Spain: "No Pasarán!" Later, she would address the International Brigades, saying: "You are history, you are legend. You are the heroic example of democracy's solidarity and universality. We shall not forget you and when the olive tree of peace puts forth its leaves entwined with the laurels of the Spanish republic's victory, come back!"

When I last saw the monument a few years ago, it had been defaced by graffiti, some of it impossible to remove. Later, the materials themselves proved inadequate to the effects of weather and fell into disrepair, the design now being examined for possible solutions.

※

The Civil War in Spain is not dead history, its themes and ideals; its failures, losses, and victories; its contemporary lessons about the way our world works—how ordinary people everywhere are caught in cyclones of political battles we are too often powerless or too frightened to affect—still pertains. Through 2015 and 2016, as I read about the forces that led up to that long-ago war, the story is hauntingly familiar:

> The military coup unleashed a series of culture wars: urban culture and cosmopolitan lifestyles versus rural tradition; secular against religious; authoritarianism against liberal political cultures; center vs. periphery; traditional gender roles versus the "new woman"; even youth against age . . .
>
> The First World War was, as elsewhere in Europe, the crucial detonator of social change. . . . The epicenter of the threat [to elite groups] was "red Barcelona." . . . But for the Spanish establishment the specter was not bolshevism but the city's powerful anarcho-syndicalist trade union movement, the CNT [committed to direct and often violent action].[5]

Part of the [Republican's] program was to separate church and state, a fundamental redistribution of power in Spain. The Catholic Church was against the Republican government from the first, considering it a "triumph of error and sin."[6]

Then came what is commonplace now, shocking, even unheard of to many then—civilians, women and children, intentionally bombed.

April 1937: Guernica, seat of the new autonomous Basque government, is destroyed by saturation bombing.

><

Silent moments passed in my father's room. Some requests for detail had been satisfied. Then Douglas—a soon-to-be lawyer whose primary love has always been history, a man whose pragmatic politics shaped by his experiences in the Civil Rights movement of the 1960s and 1970s sometimes serve, sometimes complicate his ideals—continued his quest to know more.

"And you? The International Brigades? The Republicans? You must have . . . done . . . things too?" he asked with an encouraging smile, a respectful pause.

Only recently emigrated from the South, having been beaten and jailed for sitting in at a lunch counter in Durham, North Carolina, his brother a leader of the nonviolent movement for civil rights and a conscientious objector who risked prison for refusing to fight a war against other people of color on foreign soil, Douglas's fascination with and ambivalence about the convergence of struggles for justice and use of violence lie deep in his own mind and heart. He is not a violent man by nature, not in any way or circumstance, but he is not a pacifist, as his brother was. He believes violence can be righteous and necessary, a retaliatory act. His eagerness for stories of what he felt must have included atrocities on all sides in any war was more a craving for firsthand historical knowledge than prurient interest or a desire to judge. His love for his father-in-law had grown deep during the summer of nursing him to health from the heart attack. He helped clean the old neglected apartment, prepared nourishing meals at the ancient stove, laid out ingredients on the long counter built, we were repeatedly reminded, by Steve Nelson, the heroic and famous Commissar of the Abraham Lincoln Brigade. All the domestic work Douglas managed when he returned each evening from his summer job at the law firm enabled me to leave the two of them for my classes at school. "The politics of care" the philosopher Sara Ruddick would name it in years to come, emotional intimacies so often the consequence of attentive, daily love we call "maternal."

In the early weeks of July, my father responds to his son-in-law's question with the characteristic tongue click followed by his evasive refrain: *It was war, Son* (the term of endearment meant in part to soften his refusal to give all the information he is being asked to give). *It was war, Baby*, turning to me.

Patiently, he repeats a short history of the Civil War: the border closings by France as a way of stopping the International Brigades from entering Spain; the Ebro offensive, "the greatest battle of the war." The most devastating event to the Republican cause came in September of 1938—France and Britain signed an accord with Hitler in Munich. The battle at Ebro continued, but with the loss of hope of support from Europe and America, the long conflict ended in defeat. In October, a parade of farewell to the International Brigades, flags held high, filled the streets of Barcelona, but the cause of Spanish democracy was all but defeated. In 1939, Catalonia would fall to Franco's forces; France and Britain would recognize Franco as the official head of the government of Spain. After fierce street fighting in March, fascist troops would occupy Madrid. In April, the United States would follow its allies' example and recognize the legitimacy of the fascist government in Spain.[7]

The decimations and devastations of cities and towns by Franco's forces would take years to rebuild. I can still hear my father's voice, anger mixed with undiminished sadness, responding to our questions with the now widely acknowledged truth: a dress rehearsal for World War Two—all those lives—a practice run.

As he spoke about war, atrocities on "our" side began to seem inevitable, even less horrific. Perhaps we whispered our youthful naïveté to each other late at night. Lying side by side in that room where I'd spent twenty years—most of my life at that time, only five or six years since I had left home—the clarities of my childhood in the Party were long muddied by suspicions turned to indisputable fact, my own father's health deeply compromised by the cruel denunciations of which I was still mostly ignorant. But I was clear about the mud and the mudslides, permanently affected by our loss of belief in the Party. Douglas, always more pragmatic, and thankful for a medical misdiagnosis that caused him to be rejected by the Vietnam draft, repeated my father's words about the realities of war. But we were not only allied with my father's point of view, we were struck by the obvious *presentness* of this significant part of his past.

A man whose mind could not, like some fortunate souls, file away shattering experiences and move steadily forward, wisdom gained, amputations accepted and absorbed, my father may have been remembering his own words written about Spain, the hope he tried to instill in the men remaining to fight when he himself was heading home. As I remember his recounting of experiences in 1937 many years later, I turn to some of his words from a 1938 article, "Democracy's Stake in Spain": "Returning from Spain, one frequently hears the question, 'Well how does it look in Spain? Are we going to win?'" he begins, and then answers his own rhetorical question: "The answer to the question comrades rests on: the absolute unity of all anti-fascist forces in Spain; the help the Spanish people will get from the international working class; and the help the loyalist government receives from the democratic countries in the struggle for world democracy."[8]

Further on, he writes, "Unity is a prerequisite for victory over fascism, guides its work . . . to unify all anti-fascist forces of Spain." And with characteristic hope for a broad alliance, despite his condemnation of the "Trotskyites' assassinations in Catalonia," he quotes the Manifesto of September 15 of the Party Central Committee declaring the principle of unity of all anti-fascist forces as a prerequisite to victory.

Later in his essay of appeal, he begins to tell stories:

> I shall never forget the day, while in a field hospital on the Cordoba Front, while doctors were trying to save the lives of those who required immediate operations, a battalion political commissar was brought in. He was wounded in the head. His face was beyond recognition of human features. Blood was streaming from his eyes, ears and head. He could hardly breathe. The doctor looked at him and turned away. Suddenly, while a group of us was attending to the other wounded lying beside him, we heard, "Viva Partida Comunista!" We all turned. We were stunned to realize the voice was coming from the lips of our dying Spanish comrade. We didn't look at each other—we didn't have to—but each of us knew we were all crying.

He tells the story of Rudolf Tieger, who,

> living in the trenches for weeks . . . never missed an opportunity to advance his ideas . . . in the most difficult moments making people forget their surroundings. . . . One day the order was given to go over the top. Rudolf Tieger was the first to go. He was wounded. Comrades urged him to get back into the trenches. He refused. When he finally did get back, lying there and bleeding, he remembered two of his comrades wounded, still lying in no man's land, exposed to the fire of the fascists. Slowly, with blood streaming from his head, he crawled out on his belly, brought one of his comrades into the trenches . . . he came out again, moved to the second comrade, and as he brought him close to the trenches, Tieger was riddled with machine gun bullets.

Next came the story of Henry Hines: "He was fatally wounded. As he and a group of others were being brought down on stretchers, an appeal was made to those who were lightly wounded to walk to the first aid station so that the stretchers might be used for those who could not walk. Harry Hines, the seaman, heard the appeal. He raised his head and offered his stretcher. That very moment he died."

Paying tribute to the work done in the American hospital and its ambulance crews, the "tireless enthusiasm of American doctors and nurses," he gives special mention to a name I heard repeatedly throughout my child-hood, and heard again during those evenings of the summer of 1969: Dr. Edward Barsky, volunteer, saver of lives, and, years later, still treating Communists, no doubt among other patients, in need of more ordinary medical attentions.

"We must demand," he continues, hope for support still clung to with insistent belief, "that America with its democratic traditions does not desert a bleeding nation."

I remember a tone of sorrowful nostalgia during one of those conversations: *At that time we still believed we could draw valuable lessons from Spain . . .* Did he pause for effect, silently critiquing himself yet also remembering better times, slowly repeating with recaptured energy the words he had capitalized in that essay written long before, words I am now reading again: "To work for the Peoples' Front in America!"

Despite political defeat and personal losses, he never lost a sense of the goodness of life, how to cherish moments of joy, whether momentous and glorious or small and passing. Each year on my sister's birthday and my birthday, he wrote us letters recalling his ecstasy on the days of our births, and he continued the practice in the two years in which he knew his grandson. He could glow with pleasure over a good slice of rye bread, pierced with his knife and offered around the table when company came, saving the heel for himself, just as he slurped with remembered and immediate delight his sisters' old-country cooking. He remembered so much—sometimes obsessively—reminding himself of feelings and experiences long past in silent pacing. In his silences, his expressions would shift—he'd make sounds that seemed to signal conviction, or disapproval. If someone asked, "What?" he'd usually respond enigmatically, "Just something I remembered" or "Something that came to me." His emotions rose and fell, reflected, it seemed, in a thousand songs. This quality of continual contemplation—psychological, ethical, political—perhaps rooted in some mysterious genetic wiring still unnamed—was admirable in many ways, yet could also be a source of unyielding pain, for as much as it was a sign of tireless analysis and intellectual clarity, it included at times an inability to heal. For those who loved him there was pain, too, as we listened to sometimes exhausting repetitions of his losses, or anticipated the onset of his misery in long withdrawals as he lay for hours on his bed, his face nearly hidden behind his papers and his books. We searched for instant cure, the perfect word or activity that might return him to his lively, interested self, but very often we were—I was—unsuccessful. The moods had their own rhythm, his mind its own trajectory. This combination of chronic sorrow and equally chronic energetic happiness is as familiar to me as my own face in the mirror, the memory of my own anxieties for him reflecting the anxiety I know I can cause others with this aspect of character—another part of my legacy recently entering awareness.

⸎

It was war, Dad—I must have said, echoing and supporting him during one of those summer nights while trying to support my husband's desire for *the truth*—and probably on the lookout for a story—but we want to know what *you* went through. And insisting: Tell us more about what happened there.

There was a story about nurses and doctors—one or two of them had been traitors and spies, caught injecting gangrene into the blood of Republican soldiers who would otherwise have lived. The guilty ones were not discovered and would not confess. Innocent individuals in that hospital were executed as a result. Who made that decision, if it did indeed occur? Was my father involved in it? Despite our joint pressure, he never told this story in any further detail. I have no idea if my father had any role in it if it was true; if he remained silent about it to protect others, or to protect himself, or because the story had been distorted all along, the intricacies of this distortion, like so many others at that time by pro-Franco writers and journalists working to discredit the Republican cause in Spain, too complicated or exhausting to him to begin to explain to us. I do know that the supposed atrocities attributed to the brigades continue to be debated by writers and scholars to this day. Peter Carroll quotes George Watt, Lincoln Vet and author of a memoir about his experiences in both World War Two and in Spain, as saying, "The Lincolns had not participated in the infamous atrocities in Spain."[9]

In an interview in 1983, John Murra, a Lincoln Vet and later a professor of anthropology, told of asking Nelson for advice on how to deal with deserters. Nelson replied, ". . . being a deserter isn't a permanent position. . . . Treat him like a human being." He further advised Murra "to get deserters a 48 hour pass so they wouldn't be arrested, and if possible a meal in a restaurant and a hot shower." "Overwhelmingly," Murra quotes Nelson as saying, "these men would go back to fight," which Murra found to be the truth.[10]

There was another story—about two American deserters who rather than risk sneaking without passports into France across the closed border decided to return to the base at Albacete and take their chances with the Communists. After giving them a stern lecture and warning, Commissar Lawrence advised them to return to their units—no further punishment contemplated—and so they did.[11]

❧

Who committed which atrocities, how many, and in what circumstances is beyond the scope of this story. I take my father at his word: *It was war, Baby*, and we were on the right side, on the side of justice and democracy. Which side you are on must matter. Tyranny and despotism have been recorded on all sides of most historical events and periods, but the ideas that give rise to those tyrannies, or are betrayed by them, must be included in our judgments. Franco's fascism and the ideals of those who fought against it were completely different in their vision of human beings and the societies they build. And in those words—*it was war*—many wars and testimonials later, I hear and mark also the vast difference between myself, the faraway witness, and those who are and have been on the front lines.

❧

In the autumn of 2014, my father has been dead for nearly forty-three years. On the shelf above my desk is a postcard photographed by Robert Capa in 1936—volunteers on their way to defend Barcelona. Their strong bodies lean out of the windows of the train, their fists raised in salute. I am still inspired by them, by my father's claim to the end of his life that his time in Spain remained one of his proudest experiences. I share his pride, admire his ability to salvage hope and faith out of what was at the time a devastating failure and a wrenching loss.

During those summers when we lived with him, first nursing him back to health, then counting on him for his help with our child, my thoughts repeatedly spun back through my twenty-six years to one of the central, defining myths of my life.

Spain.

He fought in Spain.

Killed in Spain.

My father fought in Spain.

No, not the Spanish American War—that was long ago, I mean the Spanish Civil War.

The Spanish Civil War? What was that?

And so, to students over many years, friends, and the younger generations, I repeat the story, and repeat it again. . . .

Volunteers came from all over the world, young men and some young women too, to fight Franco's fascists, to defend the Republic—the 15th Brigade—most of them in their early twenties. The United States Communist Party, organized, recruited, and sent many to war. Communists, young men seeking a righteous cause or merely adventure signed up to go, never expecting the carnage in store for them. American corporations like Texaco supplied oil to Franco to be used for weapons, tanks, and planes.[12] *The Catholic churches in the United States and Europe pressured governments not to intervene supporting the Catholic Church in Spain, overwhelmingly aligned with Franco and his generals. Many of the young, untrained armies of youthful idealistic soldiers who were really not soldiers at all would die.*

"Viva la Quince Brigada," we were taught to sing, our voices raised in the audience joining Pete Seeger's passionate tones as he sang the song, a familiar anthem:

Rumba la rumba, la rumba, la.
Qué se ha cubierto de gloria
ay Manuela, ay Manuela.
Luchamos contra los moros,
rumba la rumba la rum-ba-la.
Mercenarios y fascistas,
ay Manuela, ay Manuela.

Jarama. Brunete, Albacete.
Madrid.
Daddy, why do my girl cousins have boys' names for their middle names like Sidney?
And Ernest?

They were named after uncles and friends, killed in Spain.

Killed in Spain.

In the dead of night, crossing the Pyrenees Mountains on foot . . .

We heard them countless times, words and lyrics, stories and sacred phrases, siblings, cousins, friends accustomed to the multiple repetitions. Young men trekking over harsh mountainous terrain, spirit and hope driving them—*our* fathers and uncles, our close friends' fathers. The friend who lived next door to my cousin whose arm was shot through with a bullet, the hole still there, and his eagerness to show it to us, over and over: *Shot in Spain. See the hole?* He'd extend his arm so we could stare, amazed, right through the round hole to the other side, our childhood fears and disgust at the sight suppressed or at least silenced by the reality: *He fought in Spain.*

In the memoir *The Lincoln Battalion* the poet and volunteer Edwin Rolfe writes, "In Albacete, three Americans correlated the activities of all their countrymen in Spain. Their chief was Bill Lawrence, a young New Yorker with prematurely grey hair, who was American Commissar of the International Brigade Base."[13]

And at the close of chapter 1, when there is still reason for hope, he says, "The news from Spain is not too discouraging as I write these words. The Austrians are still fighting, the people of Galicia still hold out in their mountain caves, and in the steep Sierra Nevada of the south, the guerrilleros still keep the flag of the Republic and the spirit of democracy alive."

CHAPTER 8

Somewhere there is a lost letter written by my mother to my father in Spain, but I cannot find it anywhere, so I begin to wonder if I dreamed it, or made it up. She is choosing her clothes from a closet they share—a navy blue suit with a high collar and perfectly tailored sleeves. She is removing it carefully from its hanger, then she takes out a jacket that belongs to him.

But no—I must have imagined it, created it for some scene I meant to write one day. For if Bill is in Spain, they are in love but not yet married. They are not living together, certainly not in the apartment I am picturing, my childhood home. But even if they were sharing an apartment, even if it was that apartment, their room was then the one that would become mine and my sister's, the larger bedroom we were eventually to share with our grandmother. There were two closets in that room, not a single one shared, and I seem to remember my sister inherited the one that had belonged to my mother.

So, in my altered story, my mother is going through the clothes in the other closet—the one that eventually became mine, the one that belonged to her charismatic lover, a leader in the Party who had been her teacher, whose attractiveness was powerful enough for her to leave her first husband—a dark-haired, handsome man named Mike, whose photo (oddly?) remains in the old albums of my parents' early marital years. Perhaps they all remained friends. Perhaps my usually joyful, pleasure-loving mother—for most of my memories of her are of her singing, drawing with us, creating word games—was able to retain her love of a former husband even as she fell deeply in love with a new one. These memories of her clash jarringly with long periods of missing her, when she goes to work each morning in her elegant suits, when she takes a month-long trip to Paris and Italy in 1949. Finally, she is too ill for us to spend time with her in the always-dark room where she lies in a hospital bed, white sheeted, guarded by an ever-present nurse who tries to comfort her in her decline and who weeps when her beautiful suffering patient is finally gone for good.

They finally turned the lights on in that room, I would whisper to myself guiltily, sinking into angry shame. Then I'd rush to the photograph of her hanging on our wall and press my lips to the glass, swearing my love, wishing I could get to wherever she had gone. Perhaps behind the glass? For she had to be someplace.

On the back of a photograph from Spain, Bill stands at the end of a line of nine volunteers, two women in the middle, one white, one African American. He is wearing the signature béret. His hands are in his pockets, his facial expression serious and proud. On the back of the photo, he writes words that join his twin passions: *To you Tullah, I send this picture as a token of appreciation for the enthusiasm you have given me in the struggle against fascism. With love, Bill.*

><

This photograph sits on a shelf above my desk, so I can easily read my father's words. In the other letter, the one I have either lost or made up, my mother writes, "My darling Bill. I went into your closet today to feel your clothing, smell what I could of you. I put the sleeves of your favorite jacket around me, as if they were your arms, longing for you. I hope you don't think me selfish—wanting you, my darling, so much, counting the days when you will return to me, not allowing myself to imagine that you might not—but I won't even write the words. You will return. We will be together again. Republican Spain will be victorious."

Her words too come swiftly, as if from unquestionable memory—as if her letter sits on the shelf next to his note.

On the flyleaf of the book by Edwin Rolfe, its pages yellowed but not torn, its cover made of thick red cardboard so that even now as I read it once again the book is sturdy in my hands, is the inscription: *For Bill, with deepest respect and friendship, Salud y (one of these days) Victoria. As ever, Edwin Rolfe.*

And following the subtitle, "The Story of the Americans Who Fought in Spain in the International Brigades," one epigraph among several reads: *The world will little note, nor long remember, what we say here, but it can never forget what they did here. Abraham Lincoln*

From the time Douglas and I cross the border from Portugal into southern Spain, where we are to travel with a small tour for the next ten days, I begin asking our Spanish guides and other Spaniards we meet along the way about the Civil War and the monument to the International Brigades in Madrid. I have seen the photograph of the monument on line thanks to the work of the Abraham Lincoln Brigade Archives (ALBA), an organization of scholars, writers, students, those vets then still alive, and their descendants—all committed to preserving and disseminating knowledge of this critical piece of history.

But I also know of the "great silence" that followed Franco's death and the transition to democracy.

"After Franco died in 1975, *La Transición* had seemed truly miraculous. At this point, there had been no falling of the Berlin wall and no full-scale toppling of Latin American right-wing dictatorships. Nor had Spaniards, unlike their neighbors in Portugal, pushed dictatorship out with a peaceful, carnation-wielding revolution. There was no roadmap for going from authoritarian, dictatorial government to democracy. Spain was unique. It had to find its own way. And it did so by smothering the past. Truth commissions had not really yet been invented. Nuremberg-style trials of the guilty were out of the question. Many of those who would lead *la transición* had, anyway, Francoist pasts. It was better to cover their personal stories, too, with a cloak of silence. . . .

"It was unwritten, but known as *el pacto del olvido*, the pact of forgetting."[1]

✦

There is no monument, I am told again and again. *I know of no such thing*; *No, I never heard of it.* And when I press, asserting that there is indeed such a monument, adding details about the International Brigades and identifying myself as the daughter of a member of the Lincoln Battalion from America, there is only a shaking of heads, a turning away.

Then at last we meet Diego Martín, our guide through the city of Ronda, a historian who has taught in several European universities. He is the first person to mention the Civil War and the relatively recent history of fascism in Spain. A short, handsome man, somewhere between seventy and eighty years old, he is full of humor, but also with obviously prepared instructions for his audience of Americans whose naïveté he has learned to assume. I am relieved when he refers to the Civil War in his very first introductory words, and without explanation or apology informs us that Communist parties in almost every European nation sent battalions of volunteers, five international brigades known as the 15th Brigade, La Quince Brigada. He waits for skeptical or hostile response to emerge from the attentive group—but first he engenders the good feelings of comradeship that will help his real beliefs go down more easily.

A fierce rainstorm has ceased only moments before, and more rain is predicted for the afternoon of what is for the moment a sunny day. We are all dressed in rain attire, umbrellas folded into our backpacks. "Been wearing this for decades," he tells us, showing off his own worn black coat. "L.L. Bean. Best rain coat I have ever had," he says, and his reference to the well-known American catalogue company elicits the intended, comfortable smiles.

"We Andalusians love weddings, baptisms—because we love parties!" he shouts over his shoulder, expanding the feelings of cheer, then turning to face our small crowd. "We are heathens in the south of Spain. Come to us if you love parties. If you want someone to work all day, go north!" He laughs kindly at himself and at his compatriots. We all do.

But then one of our group asks, "Most of the volunteer brigades were Communists? Why were there so many Communists in the Brigades?"

"Because only the Soviet Union was supporting the Republicans," Diego responds in crisp perfect English, then, like an American Southern minister after a rhetorical flourish at the close of a speech or a sermon, he turns his back in a choreographed slide. Most likely Diego does not expect the shouts and calls of agreement the minister might count on, but I see his smile of contentment with his own words.

We follow him to several churches—churches and cathedrals being the most frequent stops on our tour through Catholic Spain. We marvel at their splendor; the ornate architecture; the altars, sculptures, and paintings; the simple elegant pews. At times I even feel a sense of spiritual calm in some of the smaller chapels, listening to strains of beautiful organ music or long echoing silence. I am affected by some of the graceful marble statues and ornately draped altars as I might be in any museum, but the history of Spanish Catholicism from the Inquisition up to the twentieth-century Civil War is never far from my mind.

As we pause to view a particularly impressive statue of a local saint, there is another question laced with suspicion: "Why so many killings and murders by the Republicans of priests and nuns?"

"Because . . ." Diego's face breaks into a by-now-familiar smile that seems to indicate, *Yes, I know these questions, they come up in every tour, and here is the answer:* "Because ninety-nine percent of the Church leaders, including local priests and nuns, were pro-Franco."

He does not encourage a reply or conversation. He has responded with the simple fact. Through the spacious rooms, down the aisles of dark polished wood we walk, Diego always ahead of us until he stops us to point out some significant painting, one an almost unbelievable depiction of the Last Supper in which all the disciples are women. "Who knows why?" he asks jovially, hands held out to emphasize the pleasures of mystery, "A feminist painter, I suppose." Then he adds, "It was also said that the priests of the time had very poor eyesight."

Finally, as in all our stops, we end up in the gift shop, where a group of tiny white stone statues are for sale—hooded figures meant to evoke ordinary monks but also inevitably suggesting the inquisitors of fifteenth-century Spain, inquisitors, we are told, who are also penitents, asking for forgiveness for pardoning the sins of the impure even while overseeing and enacting many horrific forms of humiliation and murder themselves.

"The Ku Klux Klan got their costumes from them," Diego informs us in a lowered voice, and Douglas, the only black person in our group, looks ahead with a disciplined, somewhat fierce stare while our fellow tourists cast quick, embarrassed glances his way.

A week later, on our last day in Spain, our guide will request comments from the group about our experiences. A brilliant and compassionate minister from Connecticut, with whom, along with her traveling companions, Douglas and I have formed a special friendship, will speak sadly and bravely about her sense of shame during this trip for some of the reprehensible history she has learned about the Christianity she loves. For some months after our return home, she will send us her sermons in which she boldly exposes hatreds and prejudices of many kinds, particularly policies associated with that most emblematic and long-standing American hatred—race and skin color prejudice in our institutions and our individual lives—and she preaches against the silence that helps to keep these in place. In the summer of 2014 and throughout the following year, when young black men in large numbers, suddenly newsworthy and widely discussed, are being shot and killed by American police and lone vigilantes in a number of cities, including my own, I will feel a special respect for her teachings to her Connecticut congregation, her refusal to forget.

＞＜

Of course, the Klan, like the Spanish inquisitors, hated Jews as well, and there are few Jews left in Spain.

Someone asks about the Jewish population—who were they, those large communities that once flourished here?

"Mostly they worked in the canneries," Diego responds, "until they became *conversos*, or were exiled or killed. Not many money lenders," he adds with his sarcastic smirk. "Not many professionals either. Just *workers*."

I hear his obvious socialist sympathies in the tone of respect and love he gives the last word, and behind his voice I hear my father's faithfulness to *the workers*, despite political betrayals, national and global, despite rampant racism among some white American workers he had gained an increasing ability to perceive. *Solidarity Forever*, we were taught to sing, and

The banks are made of marble, with a guard at every door,
and the vaults are stocked with silver, that the workers sweated for.

We revered union organizers like the great Joe Hill, whose famous ballad of courage and eventual murder by the "Copper Bosses" we sang at hootenannies, in the back seats of cars on family excursions, even to ourselves, humming and singing as we walked down the street or played a quiet solitary game. *I dreamed I saw Joe Hill last night*, we sang, *alive as you and me.* Most of us at that time had never left New York City, certainly never been in a mine or even a mill. Still, the words of the song came easily, as if this land were indeed our land: "From San Diego up to Maine, in every mine and mill, where workers strike and organize, that's where you'll find Joe Hill"—the lyrics of our union songs rooted and lasting in our memories— our lullabies, our inheritance.

My father's accented voice is joined by Lois's when, in her early fifties, after migrating from the South to live near her children and grandchildren in New York City, she obtained her first paying job. She received her high school equivalency degree and began a career as a civil service worker thanks to antipoverty programs in the 1970s. She began working for Head Start, complete with the salary, pension, and Social Security benefits that enabled her, when she retired and was widowed, to avoid having to depend on her children for financial support. Treasuring her union card and the benefits it accorded her from the first day on the job, she told anyone who would listen, "I'm a union member, and I tell all the rest of these suckers [her coworkers, many of whom she regarded with real affection, though they clearly had much to learn] you *got* to join the union. It's our protection." An idea she adheres to past her ninetieth year, still enjoying a collection of benefits she never expected in her first forty-five years as the wife of a professional gambler, raising a family on his steady but unpredictable income.

⤜⤛

"Workers," Diego is repeating—"Jews, Moslems, Catholics." Then, emphasizing his last word, "*Spaniards.*"

"The fascists eventually took Ronda before they moved on to Madrid," Diego tells me as we walk, and we talk about the war fought many years before, yet still so much in the atmosphere and collective psyche of Spain it has to be silenced. I write my father's two American names on a pad for him before we depart for the bus. "Yes," he says, "I think I know the name." Even if he is over eighty now, Diego was a very young child during the time my father served as base political commissar in Spain, so it may be a desire to please me more than true recognition, but whatever it is I am grateful for his loyalty to the importance of remembrance, a strong, surviving voice of refusal to *el pacto del olvido*, and I am looking forward to Madrid.

Having made our way through some of the beautiful cities and towns of southern Spain, our bus is moving through La Mancha. I am disappointed not to be seeing Albacete, where my father was stationed, but I am distracted by the numerous old windmills we can see from the windows, the kind that inspired Cervantes in his great novel and became a popular symbol of the power of illusion, but also of the grace and redemption of imagination, the dissonance between the way one is seen by others and the way one feels oneself to be. As we near the city of Toledo, I begin to sing softly the lyrics of a song written by one of my first students, many years before.

It was the early years of women's studies programs formed around the theme of women's voices liberated after centuries-long silences. Masked and disguised for many years, women had written their own stories in fiction and in poetry, but—we were all learning during that exciting time—the truth of experience was accessible if we read closely enough. Buried stories were being unearthed, reinterpreted and retold by writers, scholars, teachers, and students, new stories written from a woman's honest point of view.

My student was a Dominican woman named Pilar Brache, a brilliant poet and lyricist who, like many writers, felt that she could not find a place where she belonged; what she longed for, above all, was to be seen with love and understanding by her mother and by the world.

"I see the view from Toledo," she sang on the last day of class to us all, rapt in attention by her words and by her voice:

I see the view from Toledo . . .
And I'm sorry El Greco's my name,
I'm sorry I'm all Greek to you
Mi Madre, lo siento
Lo siento tanto.

Por eso canto.

Y canto bien.

She spoke for many of her fellow students who hoped that by finding just the right words they too might be understood, admired, confident, and known. Describing her "bilingual sadness," she translated for us: "I feel it so much"—with remarkable courage and honesty—"And so I sing. And I sing well."

Many of us, including myself, the professor of women's literature, wept.

><

As we rode down village roads and large highways that would take us to the city of Toledo, and I remembered the song and Pilar's words, claiming not only her destiny but her ability, not only her desire but her gift—some mysterious necessity to express her feelings in music and words—I kept thinking about Diego's refusal to keep the pact of forgetting. Maintaining a vow of silence, even as a way of preserving privacy or secrecy, can at times become self-betrayal—a fear of facing anger, anxiety, or shame. Perhaps I was gathering my own courage to speak out, angered by what was clearly a conspiracy of silence in Spain in 2013. I felt an internal shift of a kind I'd known before, away from repeated vows to keep strong feelings to myself in many situations—a wariness common to many aging women as our opinions and feelings are disdained or ignored. I felt the shift at first in my thoughts, scribbling notes in a travel journal I was keeping on the rolling bus, but it was to gain sound in Toledo in a situation that, though minor in a way, was nevertheless connected to the themes of communism and of the Spanish Civil War.

><

In what is described as the most important cathedral in Spain, we are surrounded by marble bishops and saints, all created by artists who were sponsored by the Church. There are enough gold, silver, and precious gems in this church, we are told by one museum guide (perhaps off the record?) to feed the entire country, and as I gaze at the riches displayed before me, I recall the words of our primary guide through Spain, Rosa of Catalonia, speaking to us from her front seat on the bus earlier that day.

In Spain now, she had told us all, insisting on our attention as we rode down highways and gorgeous tree lined country roads, there is an economic disaster, "The Crisis," as it is referred to by everyone in Spain. Mass unemployment; high rents even outside the cities; people in their twenties and thirties returning home to live with parents; grandparents taken out of nursing homes so their government income—"like your social security," Rosa explained—can help to support the family. Many have to live on four hundred euros a month, yet the average mortgage is seven hundred a month. Many immigrants have begun to return to their home countries. Retirement age has been increased, salaries decreased. In the hotel where we stayed the night before, she said, standing and facing us from the front of the bus, holding the microphone close to her chest, her voice modulated with only partial success, one worker she knew was managing four jobs to keep his family fed. I could see it took courage for Rosa to make this speech, even to a group of tourists she knew fairly well by now and seemed to like. It was not on the agenda. Like Diego, she was making waves.

Throughout this writing, I have been invoking my father's teachings, the *values* he insisted on at every opportunity, but also his courage, even as a young man on trial, then, later, speaking out not only to political enemies and government officials, to whom he wrote weekly letters approving or disapproving of their votes, but to former comrades, to family, friends, and—especially—to his daughters. As Rosa instructed us about the realities of economic suffering in the Spain we are admiring as tourists—eating well, sleeping in comfortable lovely rooms, our beds made and our bathrooms cleaned by someone else—my father's voice and principles interrupt my journey again.

The shift announces itself first as a mild nausea. In a room adjoining the nave of the church, a kind of gallery leading to the sanctuary, we find walls lined with paintings by El Greco. The brilliant rose pinks and dark greens of the holy robes temporarily overshadow the metaphor Pilar made of him and his famous work, yet I am unable to banish thoughts of the vast inequalities of wealth growing in the United States. In my own home of Manhattan, rents from the Bowery to Harlem now reach levels that make it impossible for even middle-class families to live there. Local stores owned by people who have become neighbors, part of a familiar community, are closing daily, replaced by banks and huge drugstore chains—the only ones who can afford the rents, I was told only the previous week by a long-known store owner preparing to move. Billions of dollars go into maintaining a vast and punitive criminal justice system, but sufficient money for education can somehow never be found.

I walk around the room, humming Pilar's lyrics, lost in the intensity of the whites, reds, blacks, and greens that dominate the portraits of political and religious leaders of the time. But I am growing slightly dizzy. I close my eyes partly, representational outlines dimming as I try to remain in a fluid world of color, shape, and spreading light, leaving more disturbing thoughts temporarily behind—just as in another country, in another beautiful place, I might dive into a high-tide bay to swim, letting the rhythm of my body and breath free me of somber thoughts and anxiety. But the diving won't hold. The dizzy nausea persists. The real subject of my meditations will resurface very soon.

We leave the church, the El Grecos, my memories of a young artist's voice, and are led down winding, cobbled streets to the Jewish Museum. All of us are Americans, ranging in age from late forties to eighty. Including myself, there are four Jews in a group of about twenty-five. Here, Rosa takes a break and we are led by a local guide who stands in the midst of our circle in a central room surrounded by hallways and galleries. Lining the walls are glass cases filled with magnificent artifacts from the thriving synagogue this place was many years earlier.

When there were Jews living on what is still called Calle de Judios (Jew Street or Street of the Jews), these rooms would have been gathering places for daily worship, holy days, sermons, bar mitzvahs, weddings, funerals—all the aspects of community life religion can provide. It is beautifully preserved, but there are no Jews here. They were killed, expelled, or converted during the Inquisition in the 1400s, or they escaped to northern Europe, where they thought they were safe, but where five centuries later they would be murdered and tortured, sent to concentration camps, millions to their deaths.

My mind and eyes are wandering. I even leave the group to gaze at silver wine goblets, enormous ornate menorahs, a large scroll of the Torah, its ancient pages of Hebrew lettering conveying a sense of sacred history, if not religious holiness, to my agnostic soul—the black lines, shapes, and dashes of the letters themselves beautiful to me, even if I do not understand them as words.

When I wander back to the group, listening half attentively to yet another interesting but repetitive description of architecture and icons, I am
suddenly shocked into attention. The pleasant local guide, whose curly
brown hair and multicolored shawl I have admired throughout the hours
in Toledo, is defending the Inquisition. "It was wrong, of course," she tells
us in perfect English, her tone clearly asserting it was not so completely
wrong—it is complicated, more to come, more to understand—her hesi-
tant tone clearly conveys a "but."

"You must understand," she continues, "King Ferdinand and Queen Isa-
bella had many pressures on them," and the contemporary phrase completes
the warning. We wait for what inevitably will follow, and very soon it does.
"There have been many injustices all over the world," she lectures in a voice
that now exudes resentment and anger. "Why should only Spain's failings
be so condemned, even exaggerated? Look at your own country," she says,
her voice louder now. "What about the Salem witch trials? Were they not
as evil as anything done here?"

One of the Jewish women in our group is deeply observant. She immediately leaves the room.

So I speak up, my own voice loud to match the guide's. "What you are
saying is offensive and insulting," I manage to say, ignoring the ever-present
voices counseling silence—*what's the difference?*—knowing the foolishness
and futility of any response, but I am not stopping, "especially standing
here in this synagogue-turned-into-a-museum, because there are no Jews left
here. At least not many. But there are four of us here, in this room right now,
and we four, maybe the others too, are outraged by your words."

Then I walk out into the air. Later, I learn that Douglas has continued
for me, pointing out the absurdity of the example of the Salem witch trials
in which twenty or so people were killed, however brutally and unjustly,
comparing it to the expulsion and murder of tens of thousands of Jews from
Spain, especially considering the long, recent history of deadly European
anti-Semitism. Standing with him and a few of the others on the narrow
Street of the Jews in Toledo, breathing deeply to restore myself to calm, I
remember a section from George Charney's book about conflicts between
ethnic and internationalist identities.

In the 1940s, Party members in New York were predominantly Jewish, and by the 1950s, exposures of anti-Semitism in the Soviet Union became well known and condemned, even among Communists.

"As an American Jew I had become a communist, and in time these parts of my social being had become fused," George wrote. "Now the unity had been shattered."[2]

Fierce debates within the Party followed, American-born Communists often pitted against "the older foreign born generation like Bill," wrote George, who had come to this country as a child. "I would think of my Jewish origins, the emotions engendered by the plight of the Jews in Europe, the epic of the Warsaw ghetto, and know with certainty that whatever my political beliefs now or in the future, I was a Jew." During one debate, "Bill Lawrence took the floor, the only occasion on which he spoke," George writes, and he quotes him as saying, "I too have Jewish blood in my veins. I also have communist blood!"—in "ringing tones."

George interprets his old friend's words as indicating a failure to see and accept that Communists could be guilty of such appalling crimes as have now been indisputably revealed. And certainly the wish to deny may have been part of my father's resistance. But standing on the lovely cobblestone street outside the Jewish Museum of Toledo in 2013, I thought about that internationalist identification that remained so primary for him. A few years later, when his relation to the American Party would be broken forever, that belief would still supersede ethnic origins and the Jewish identity that felt intrinsic to his very being since his earliest years as a child in the Jewish quarter of Kishinev.

As in many other places and times, including in our present time, Franco's obsession with purity, in his case a *pure* form of Catholicism, was used as justification for exile and murder. At this point in history the very concept of ethnic and racial purity has been revealed not only as myth but as one of the most pernicious aspects of religions, a powerful source of violence against differences of all kinds. I knew this in 1968 when I married a black man in an America where, despite the 1967 decision by the Supreme Court in the case of *Loving vs. The State of Virginia* that made "interracial" marriage legal in the nation, it was still kept on the books as illegal in most states; when I spent most of my life raising black sons whose very "mixedness" made them a threat to much of white America. I had spoken up for them, learned from them, written and taught about the damage and brutal impact of the false idea of pure whiteness, a political and social concept that rests on forces more complex than single issues of heritage, religious belief, skin color, or ethnicity. Traveling through Spain, the International Brigades seemed more than ever to represent a commonality of values preempting national borders and backgrounds, intrinsically interwoven with principles of economic justice—a beautiful alternative, still far from achieved. "I was politicized my whole life," recalled Ruth Davidow, a nurse who had gone to Spain to protest Roosevelt's policy of nonintervention, "but when I got to Spain . . . I learned what international solidarity meant."[3]

Speaking out in one small place against one foolish woman expressing an excuse for the ideology of purity at the heart of the Inquisition, Spanish fascism, American racism, and eventually the Holocaust is a minor act, I know, not risky or apt to change anything at all. But I continued to feel that small clarifying shift within. Vowing *not to forget* can never be a vow hidden in silence, but needs an audible, visible claim—like Pilar's lyrics, like Diego's purposeful guidance, like paintings and voices yet to come in our journey through Spain—needs sound, images, words.

><

In the now beautifully restored streets and boulevards of Madrid, Douglas and I walk through parks and visit museums, and I try to imagine those broad inviting avenues as mountains of debris and demolished buildings, bodies of the dead and wounded lying everywhere, as my father would have seen them in the 1930s, as we had witnessed on television that morning the bleeding, severed bodies lying among large broken stones that once were homes in the streets of Syria.

In the Museo Nacional Centro de Arte Reina Sofía, we stand with dozens of others before Picasso's *Guernica*. I had seen it years before at the Museum of Modern Art in New York, but here in Madrid, with the painting's history of exile and return to Spain only at the death of Franco, it takes on a more powerful aura than ever before. The screaming faces, women in shouted lament holding dead children, animals broken into severed heads and lost limbs, sharp triangular weapons seeming to be parts of destroyed homes, a pathetic lightbulb shining white and gray over the darkness of shades of black—the painting seems to possess sound as well, and we crowd with many others viewing the depiction of this moment of historical carnage that has become a symbol of so much carnage to come.

In the Prado, exhausted by travels through space but also through time, we decide to visit only one gallery—the somber exhibit of Goya's *Black Paintings*.

All is quiet in these rooms. Faces of starving workers, desperate pilgrims, destitute peasants, lurid murders and dismemberments stare out at us. *Saturn Devouring One of His Children* is monstrous, frightening, compelling. The printed text and published brochures describing the formal achievements but also the historical interpretations of these works give rise to thoughts of Spain's current "Crisis," Rosa's grim statistics about poverty and unemployment, Diego's reminders of the brutal effects of inequality. Dense yet miraculously translucent blacks and browns, sudden streaks of red—all seem to reflect the violent years of civil war and the decades of fascist dictatorship that followed.

The previous morning, we had taken a tour of a famous castle, but I found myself without any enthusiasm to admire the aesthetics of massive crystal, gold and silver artifacts, utensils and furniture patterned with sapphire, emerald, and ruby surrounded by circles of silver and gold. I kept seeing lines of refugees as if they were trekking down the wide gorgeous halls, not only from the past during the Civil War here, but those we had seen on the news the night before, homeless and grief-stricken, carrying sick children to huge makeshift camps. They are marching all over North Africa and the Middle East, their numbers soon to reach into the hundreds of thousands as they penetrate the borders and nations of Europe. Their faces are lined and gray, creases embedded with dust, children's eyelids closing on flies. Increasing nausea forced me out of the building and into an interior garden, opulent too, but outside at least, where I breathed fresh air.

Filled to our tolerance with the anguish of history, we shared memories of conversations with my father forty years earlier. We found rest and refreshment in the lovely open cafés and tapas bars. We walked off our conflicted emotions of admiration for this beautiful city and recent studies of its disturbing yet at times inspirational history, a history that will always influence our own, our children's, and our granddaughter's lives.

When Adam was only one year old, my father gave him a silver medal: "Friend of the Abraham Lincoln Brigade," its tiny raised letters read. Then he wrote one of his customary letters, briefly describing for his grandson the history of the war, and his own participation in it. "I am sure," he concluded, "that had you been around in those days you would have been a true friend of the Abraham Lincoln Brigade. Keep it as a memento, and once in a while you can even wear it."

＊＜

But our primary concern here in Madrid has always been the monument.

The tribute to the International Brigades was on the campus of the Universidad Complutense de Madrid where many died defending the city. We were warned by guides, the hotel concierge, and others we met along our way to be prepared. The university professor (unnamed) who finally got the monument built "did not pay enough attention to politics," so there has probably been some vandalism, perhaps insulting graffiti at the least, they caution us.

We travel to the university alone one morning, the others on our tour busy with other interests. It is Easter week, so the campus is deserted as we search for the student center where the monument supposedly stands. Lost at first in the intertwining paths and grass quadrangles, we finally find two young security guards, and in my minimal Spanish I ask them if they know the location. I describe the background as best I can. With my hands and arms I draw an invisible picture of a tall statue in the air. Douglas is wearing his old, worn black béret—an ordinary one, certainly not the Lincoln Battalion béret that sits on a shelf in our younger son's apartment in New York—but the hat must trigger the idea, and the words are finally spoken in Spanish and English—the Monument to the International Brigades in the Civil War. *Yes, sí, that is what we look for.* One of the men looks at us with sudden fascination and asks Douglas if he is a veteran of the brigade. Instantly, he realizes his mistake, that Douglas is much too young, but then I am able to find the words to introduce myself—*una hija*—a daughter of a volunteer and, interested, the guard pulls out his iPhone, quickly finds the picture we have seen on our own computers at home, and points out the directions to its location.

But we are already there, right where the Google map describes, and when we look up from the guards, across the lawn, there it is—the monument itself. We all laugh—our reliance on virtual technology blinding us to actual life—and with many thanks, Douglas and I rush across the green.

In front of La Casa del Estudiante and Centro Internacional de Visitantes y Acogida (a meeting place, or shelter for visitors) a narrow stone obelisk rises up before us. It was established, the plaque at its foot reads, by the "Asociación de Amigos de Las Brigades Internacionales," and "Comisión Internacional de Deseño." It was paid for by private donations to memorialize the hundreds of International Brigaders who died in Madrid.

Etched into the monument beneath a large triangle of red stone is written,

A Los Voluntarios de Las Brigades Internacionales.
22-X-2011

And beneath those, additional words:

Sois la historia, sois la leyenda
Sois el ejemplo heroico de la
solidaridad y de la universalidad de la democracia.

Then, an engraved signature: "Dolores Ibarruri 1-xi-1938" (La Pasionaria, the fighter known for her leadership and courage, the spiritual voice of the Republic).

I walk around the slim monument many times, my fingers tracing the metal that reflects the light of the afternoon. Years before, I had visited the Western Wall in Jerusalem and, according to the custom of inserting private handwritten prayers into the crevices between the stones, I'd left a plea for peace in my parents' and my children's names. In Madrid, I slip a paper into a tiny crevice at the base of this memorial: *Greetings and salud de Bill Lawrence, Political Commissar of the Abraham Lincoln Brigade, 1937.*

Though I know it will fade with the next rain, I inscribe a large flat stone with a penned message: "Viva la Quince Brigada. Abraham Lincoln Battalion. De una hija de uno voluntario."

As I lay a stone on a narrow ledge at the base of the monument, as you would lay a stone marking your visit on the edge of the tombstone of a Jewish grave, I thought about how in the years after the war so much would fall apart for my father. The need for alliances during World War Two and the Popular Front ideology that had dominated Soviet perspectives and international parties would be discredited and condemned. Many would be murdered, executed, and imprisoned in the Soviet Union, and here among the American comrades, many, like Bill, would be denounced into political and spiritual exile, their faith shaken in many cases, in many their health destroyed. It had begun long before, back in the 1920s, when Bill lived in Philadelphia, worked in a textile factory, became an American organizer for the Party, was imprisoned for "attempting to overthrow the government of Pennsylvania," and eventually moved to New York.

In my files and notebooks at home I had a large collection of material about those early years, documents, articles, on my bookshelves numerous books by participants and observers, devotees and harsh critics, loyal comrades to the end and those who had denounced their former beliefs and the Party they felt had betrayed them, and I looked forward to the research awaiting me, reading that would assume a new reality having seen Spain with my own eyes.

I had a history teacher in high school whose words I think of often as they pertain to my life in so many realms, from the broadest political forces that affect my various commitments to my most intimate relationships. Before every new unit she would intone in a voice so loudly projected we were surprised to hear it emanating from the small and very ordinary-looking woman who stood before us in the room. Leaning back on her desk, her arms crossed across the high-buttoned white or flowered blouse enclosing her narrow torso, she would say, "Now we will go back and study causes, both obvious and underlying forces at work, and then we will come to understand consequences. In history nothing happens without the thing that happened before."

✦

Two months after our return home from Spain, the memorial would be removed by order of the Supreme Court of Madrid, claiming the proper planning permission had not been obtained. In November, 2015, forty years after the death of Franco and a return to a democratic republic, the *New York Times* would report that many streets and monuments still bear the names of Franco as well as other well-known fascists. "The shadow of Franco continues to be a potent source of division between right and left," the reporter Raphael Mendes would write. But there is no other plaque or memorial to the International Brigades in the entire city of Madrid.

PART IV   *A Bad Wind*

. . . this we were, this is how we tried to love,
and these are the forces they had ranged against us,
and these are the forces we had ranged within us,
within us and against us, against us and within us.

ADRIENNE RICH, *XVII*, "TWENTY-ONE LOVE POEMS"

I call it a bad wind when it happens to me—months, once a few years of consecutive losses, not all of them tragic but all of them severe. A bad wind swept through my father's life. It began soon after the end of World War Two, its velocity increasing steadily to hurricane levels, ending in a need for abdominal surgery, medications not yet discovered, to remove an ulcer. Was it bleeding? His heart was bleeding, his heart was broken, his mind endangered by shattering splits if he did not use all of the self-control he had always valued and often achieved.

I visited him in the hospital early one evening in 1959 before the start of my "sweet sixteen" party. I was wearing a shiny gold dress, its skirt made stiff and wide by thick layers of the cotton lace crinolines popular at the time. Beautiful and punishing high-heeled shoes made my chronic foot problems worse—I could hardly walk straight—but when the dancing started later that night, I danced barefoot much like all the other girls, bending backward in my boyfriend's arms, down on bent knees as I passed through his opened legs. The stiff girdles we all still wore to flatten our stomachs were also removed by then. I felt graceful and free.

But my father's face had been disturbingly pale, almost as gray as the grayish-white hospital sheets. Tubes emerged from his nose and mouth, his voice was low and scratchy from the anesthesia and medications, maybe also from his tears, scratching my feelings as storm-swept gravel can scratch and hurt your feet.

"Poles and Russians knew how hidden feelings poisoned life," Alan Furst writes in *Dark Star*,[1] and though my father was never in much danger of that particular poisoning, you could see him trying.He rallied, he smiled, he removed the mouth tube to whistle and told me I looked beautiful. "Have a wonderful time, Sweetheart," he gravel-whispered, the merged *v/w* making a birthday gift for me—its familiarity, his survival. But I knew the tears were there too, we always knew, our mother's ghost lurking in the air, the words *If only your mother could see you now* always there, the *if only* evaporated like damp mist dried to nothing by hot sun. She was there in his never-ending wish, ruining sometimes momentarily, sometimes for longer, every occasion or celebration, his evocation meant in some part of his broken heart as love.

The bad wind began in 1948 and continued through the 1950s.

><

Between the end of World War Two in 1945, and the end of the decade, the international Communist movement and leaders were in a conflict sufficiently cruel to be lethal in the end to the movement as a whole.

In 1944, Earl Browder, longtime chairman, had dissolved the "Party" and reconstituted it as the Communist Political Organization, reasserting, in contrast to the idea of the revolutionary elite with its organizational center in the Soviet Union, the value of alliances with democratic organizations and progressive unions, a strategic and philosophical commitment to connect national organizations in a movement for radical social change. My father was an ally of Browder's. They worked together in the 1940s, and had jointly written articles about Spain. But by 1945 what George Charney calls "the old dilemma of the relationship of ideology and party to nationality" was about to explode into long simmering factions, deepening suspicion in an atmosphere of denunciation and accusation across the Communist movement with its origins in Soviet Stalinism.[2]

Vague memory altered by childhood fears and wishes pass through my mind like sea clouds as I try my hand at historical discourse. The details of arcane battles and divisions on the Left of that time move into focus through the words of a writer I have learned to trust for his fairness and clarity.

"In the end," writes Peter N. Carroll in *The Odyssey of the American Lincoln Brigade*, "a new leadership committed to orthodox Leninist formulas forced Browder's expulsion . . . just at the time that an anti-Communist crusade was beginning [in the US]."[3]

Returning to George Charney's "journey" through his years as an American Communist is more like the granting of an impossible wish than research itself—as if this almost uncle were still alive, smoking his pipe in his living room, surrounded by his shelves of books, his short gray hair and pedagogical conversations—the sense of him—nearly as familiar to me as my own father. He was one of the Communist fathers closest to my heart, many of them kind and affectionate, appreciative of their own and each other's daughters. Our intelligence, what they saw as our beauty, even when we were less than beautiful, their insistence on our need to be educated and respected—this form of love was no less welcomed for its imperfections. Despite instances of outright sexism, they grappled with "the woman question" in serious ways.

I think the daughters got the best of them—the sons, grown now into aging men, seem and seemed since our youth to be more damaged. Fathers and sons, often embattled, were embattled in our world too as paternal expectations clashed with adolescent identities and young male assertion—all played out as always against the background of history—the struggle for civil rights, the Vietnam War. Daughters in our world, like many other daughters, were more apt to forgive fathers, to adore them far more than mothers, whose tasks and responsibilities reached beyond and much closer in than philosophical and political instruction, or to a special evening out to see a current Broadway show whose song lyrics tilted to the Left, or an excursion to Wollman's ice skating rink with its delicious pizza and romantic music.

By both nature and circumstances, Bill was an exception to this pattern in some ways—choosing a domestic center for his single-parent life. But the other fathers, George central among them, still carry a scintillating aura of charisma years after their deaths, an indelible memory of their integrity and our trust.

✦

During the years Charney describes as a "time of upheaval," Jacques Duclos, a French Communist theoretician, published a letter read by all as a text from Stalin himself. In it, he denounced recent "revisionist tendencies" and summoned a return to the "class struggle."[4] Responding to this cue, the American Party hierarchy, by then led by the doctrinaire William Z. Foster and war hero Bob Thompson, pressed Browder to renounce his program and—to them—his dangerous assertion that progressive forces allowing for a peaceful development toward socialism existed within the system of capitalism in the United States. The idea of an international elite was resurrected. The united front ideology was now deemed corrupt.[5]

Knowing that at times my reading is braided with memories of anger and love, at other times with the inevitable prejudices of perspective and belief of any writer, I am careful of too much confidence in my impressions, let alone any certainties. But as I read and write, trying to sift new knowledge from old assurances, I do know this: When beliefs turn religious and discordant opinions become a source of righteous hatred, violence of many kinds, physical and verbal, may erupt. This can be as true in personal, intimate life as in the political arena. The overlapping of these supposedly separate spheres has long been revealed as two aspects of one human experience, though it would be decades before my generation of feminists simplified the idea into four now famous words—the personal is political—a concept the postwar Communists, among others, were still able to deny. For those now in power, battle positions assumed a crusade-like righteousness, unmitigated by ambiguity or doubt, unsoftened by compassion for previous friendships, the capacity to think clearly or accurately observe finally dimming into full obliteration. Hatred reigned. Many were sacrificed, charged with "revisionism," "opportunism," and "political deterioration."

Describing an experience of encountering two men at a Party conference, one a respected comrade, one his old friend, George Charney writes,

> Bob Thompson and Bill Lawrence—the new and the old, and each gave his own interpretation of events. Bob represented the Party and had spoken with supreme confidence . . . [having] spent half of the previous decade in combat, first in Spain, then in the South Pacific, [he] stood at the summit, the personification of the Vanguard. Bill spoke for himself alone and with dark misgivings about the future. . . . He had been an inspiration in the 30s, . . . [but now] those who had assumed leadership positions regarded him with indifference or ill-concealed contempt, as though he belonged to the past. . . . The attacks came from all quarters during the

endless convention sessions. I could picture him seated in the front row, the butt of harsh criticism, his head bowed, unable or unwilling to defend himself. The most crushing blow came when a Lincoln Veteran threw in some snide, cruelly unjust remark about his conduct in Spain. . . . So my friend Bill had fallen.[6]

⊁⊰

On December 2, 1948, shortly before eight in the morning, Bill's older brother, Buck, political comrade and close friend since their youth in Kishinev and Philadelphia, died suddenly of a heart attack. I remember his blue eyes, common to the Lazarre side of my family, his thick white hair, his face resembling my father's in its pale tan and pink skin tones, but less craggy, handsomer, I would now say, staring at their photograph framed on my wall. He visited us often, played with my sister and me on the floor of the living room. Once, I suddenly remember, he brought us a set of building blocks shaped like men, some green, some blue, some red—perhaps there was a single white one, a black one—I think so, and each with a few black lines indicating the features of a smiling face. They were made so you could build a tower, each one standing on the shoulders of another. A children's game designed for Communist families? Could that be? Or just a clever version of ordinary blocks my uncle found in some store and with my father interpreted as representations of the beliefs we all shared: strong men, *working men*, all standing together. If you pulled one out from the structure, all the rest would fall.

I have no idea if this interpretation of the men-blocks is memory or if it just occurs to me as a possibility now. Images are surfacing as if from an especially vivid dream, and I cherish memories like this one, for happiness can fade too easily with the multiple traumas that dominated those years.

I see my father's signature on his brother's death certificate in my now large collection of documents. Isaac Lazar's profession is listed, falsely of course, as "instrument maker." Perhaps it was a simple fib, Communists in the ingrained habit of lying about their work lives during those dangerous years. Or perhaps even at his brother's deathbed, my father was being sardonic. *Instrument maker.* The Party had often been known as the "Instrument of the Revolution" and of the eventually victorious working class. And

Buck had been a leading theoretician of the Party. He was single at the time of his death, only forty-nine years old. He died at Mount Sinai Hospital in Manhattan, where in the year following, my mother would be treated for the breast cancer that would slowly kill her. I read her certificate of death, also signed by William Lazar, as a lamentation of remembered grief.

It would be many decades later when, with Douglas and my son Khary, I would make another journey to my mother's and uncle's graves in that Long Island cemetery and feel the beginning of peaceful closure. The section where their gravestones stand is entered through a stone arch in which are inscribed the words: *They lived not for themselves alone.*

CHAPTER 11

I have a recurring dream of a dark city. Human shapes fade into shadows. It seems to be the far western side of Manhattan, avenues that long before the Chelsea piers were opened led to the docks where ocean liners from Europe came in, where my father—twice I think—but it may have been only once—took my sister and me to wait for my mother's return from a business trip to Paris. But then the familiar city fades, and I am in a foreign place, reminiscent of photographs of cities in the old country decades earlier—not a large, metropolitan city but a small, ancient-seeming neighborhood. The darkness of the nighttime street near the river stretches into a tiny cluster of houses and from there into forests and hills. A bus is heading toward the river, a tributary of the open sea where the ocean liners dock. Above me large elevated structures move into the distance, like the train tracks on upper Broadway in Manhattan, or long, curving bridges connecting one thing to something else. Some of the wood is crumbling. Other parts are sturdy, apparently unbreakable, made of steel. So the two places overlap, or are somehow the same.

My dreams are vivid, like most dreams filled with sudden shifts and strange juxtapositions. They are and always have been almost daily morning experiences, coming to me as I wake as if I have literally been somewhere else. Characters and places recur and develop—as they might in waking time.

Partly for this reason, I became aware very early in my life of worlds within me beyond consciousness and control. During this time, at about the age of eighteen, searching for ways to dispel anxiety and fears, sometimes presenting themselves as "voices"—a sense of splitness that convinced me for years I was a "crazy person," just as my grandmother had always warned—I became passionate about psychoanalysis. But I was not only seeking relief or "cure" in my years as a patient and student of this ever-revising theory of the mind. I was drawn to the narrative of liberation elaborated by generations of psychoanalysts more or less indebted to Freud. First secretly, then in open debate with my father, I believed that the idea of interior freedom must be related to his lifelong dedication to social and political freedom for all people. Still, the idea at the heart of psychoanalysis, that subjugation and tyranny could be partially rooted in early childhood experience, as well as in systems of governments, filled him with anger verging at times on contempt I now see as a sign of dread.

I know only the bare outlines of my father's childhood. Neither I nor my sister nor any of our cousins knew his parents. Both died shortly after their arrival in America, and though my father spoke often of his hated father, never admitting to any form of attachment let alone love, he talked little of the grandmother with whom he slept until the age of five. Nor did he tell many stories of his mother, but he called her "Mama" when he spoke of her, never the more emotionally distant "my mother," and when he occasionally referred to her early death, the easy tears came. There was one story from their early days in Philadelphia. When his father died, he and his brother Buck promised their mother to go each morning to synagogue to say Kaddish, but instead, fervent and righteous young Communists, they went to a coffee shop and talked about the future of the world. I don't recall him ever expressing regret for what must have seemed to his mother a betrayal and a *shanda*—a disgrace, a great shame—and he never said where she or his father were buried. But he never visited my mother's grave either, an uncompromising materialist in this question of the body and the soul. When my father wrote his last wishes for us, he left strict instructions (which I disobeyed) to throw his cremated ashes onto the back of a garbage truck. This belief, of course, did not diminish loss or ameliorate his grief. I see him sitting at the large kitchen/dining room table having just heard of yet another loss—the death of his eldest sister, Leza—and as he wept he repeated,

"She was to me like a second mama," the new loss, as always, slicing open the wound of the old.

In the old-country lament he crooned each night after our mother died when he took over the bedtime ritual of a song before sleep, I lay in bed trying to sink into always elusive surrender while he sang about a dark night—*nacht in droysen*—and a child who is left to wander narrow streets without his mother—*nit kine mama*—a sign of convergence where our stories crossed. ("Please, not *nacht in droysen*," I'd plead, pronouncing the words all wrong but knowing what I didn't want to hear, though night after night that is what I got.)

He is forty-eight years old in 1951 when my mother dies closely following his brother's death, both on the heels of the Party's transformations and betrayals. His friendship with George Charney broke apart for some years as a result of political differences that landed them on opposing sides of the Party. Alliances were rapidly shifting, the participants moved around, belief turned into its opposite even within one person, then rigidified again, internal enemies more demonized, it can seem now, than the "armies" of external threat to international socialism.

In a chapter in which George castigates himself for his failure to defend his friend Bill from the new Party regime in which George himself has now become a leader, I find this description: "I met my friend Bill Lawrence. . . . I was appalled by his appearance. He was ashen and lifeless, he who had always spoken with such a splendid, flamboyant air. . . . I was shaken by his interpretations of the upheaval in the party. . . . It was clear . . . that in the course of the upheaval some people, among them Bill, had suffered the tortures of the damned . . . under circumstances that left him isolated and alone."[1]

Then between the ages of seven and nine, I was entangled within my own chaos, trying to comprehend death itself, memories of my mother outlined in splendor then shrouded in ragged despair, filling me with guilty rage. I recall my father's double image, always shifting. The charismatic and powerful revolutionary, full of humor and easy old-world affection, dressed in his pressed blue suit and starched white shirt when leaving our apartment for work, as if he were headed for the stock broker firm we had learned to lie about when asked by strangers what he did for a living. And the man who was shattered, in the grip of an increasing depression that would stalk him on and off until his death. Now the old splits knit together and it is obvious that the double image is a false one; he was always one man encompassing oppositions, strengthened by the same passions that broke him in the end.

Bill and George reconciled soon after my mother's death, and George, then secretary of the New York State Party, enabled a partial redemption for his old friend, who as a section organizer had recruited him years earlier. Bill had disciplined and taught him—though once, then on somewhat different sides of the old repetitive argument, Bill had criticized George for omitting the phrase "for a Soviet America" from a pamphlet designed to recruit American workers to attend a rally—he had recognized George's brilliance and his dedication. Their reconciliation was partly due to the fact that George's wife Hattie had been friends with my maternal aunt since their college days and had known my mother since she was a child. It was certainly important that the families were close, the children in some ways raised more as siblings or cousins than as friends. George had much to lose in losing Bill. So when their respective power positions in the Party reversed, George in favor with the new regime, Bill discarded as part of the old, George found a way to retain Bill in a succession of compromised and diminished positions. The last of these was Director of the Cultural Region.

CHAPTER 12

Commissar of the Cultural Region. Do I remember that title from my father's often ironic humor, or did I dub him so myself, by then a clever daughter using words to woo and enrage him, his demotion a humiliation for him but one that unexpectedly would save my own life?

I was introduced to a large group of artists, many of them my father's students, active rank-and-file members or at least "fellow travelers," painters, writers, actors, gathering regularly in our living room to talk and debate party policy and Marxist, Leninist texts. As the 1950s moved on and McCarthyism began to take hold of the nation, some were already blacklisted, in danger of losing or already having lost their access to work. I lay in bed listening to them argue into the night, or I sat enraptured when we visited them in spacious apartments on Central Park West, an uptown world that was as exotic to my life in Greenwich Village as years later my home would be to my high school friends from the Bronx. These men and women saw me differently than I had been seen before. Like my then still future stepmother, they seemed (I would later find this "seemed" to be true when, as a young adult, I had long and illuminating talks with some of them) to find me recognizable, within a world of double outsiders—artists and Communists—even ordinary. This ordinariness was medicinal to me, who had always been defined as a difficult, chronically incomprehensible child. I relished its opening to relationship. They appeared to think I was perfectly normal, and I wanted to be like them.

I learned to cue the actors for a coming part; I painted self-portraits and carefully arranged still lifes in the studio of Gladys, the beautiful, dark-haired artist (one of my father's "friends") I visited every Saturday to prepare a portfolio—gorgeous new word—for the test for the High School of Music and Art in Harlem; I was fascinated by the stories some of the writers told so fluently, humorously, and meaningfully—smiles and frowns pointing to hidden messages, careful pauses and wonderfully strange vocabulary evoking vivid scenes spreading into lengthy narratives, all told around large food-laden tables. I found myself in a new world of rich and various possibilities, beckoning choices within the world of Art.

New objects, enticing skills, previously undreamed of possibilities.

Oil paint and turpentine, linseed oil and palettes—not the small wooden ones I had known in children's paint boxes but large slabs of glass with every tone of every color lined up around the border, a wide space in the middle for mixing and blending into gorgeous subtle shades. One of those heavy, frosty slabs was lent to me for all the time I studied in that well-lit room packed with canvases, several easels, large tubes of paint, huge jars of brushes of various shapes and grades of silk. There, kept on a shelf with my name written across the front, was my palette, my box of paints, my palette knife, and, against the wall of stacked canvases, my canvas, stretched and half done: *a work in progress*. As I thought about my painting between lessons, I was careful to keep a keen eye on drawings one of the artists might swiftly sketch of the faces around a dinner table, eyes suggested in thick black charcoal strokes yet looking like real eyes, noses distinct and individual, not the half moon arcing over two holes I called a nose in my attempts at portraits, and hair of every grade and shape, made vivid with a few graceful circles or lines. Mentally, I listed techniques, planned to perfect what I had painted the week before, eyed certain pencils so hungrily, I guess, that several were offered to me to keep as my own.

In the small, crowded apartment of the *real* actress my father would soon marry, costumes were kept in large trunks and baskets as tall as myself, long skirts and fringed shawls, satin robes and feathered hats, in which we dressed when enacting improvisations, the intriguing beginning of stories filled with secrets whispered to each performer separately, no one knowing how, or if, the secret would be revealed before our actor/director called for the scene to end. People I knew in real life actually appeared on stage becoming someone else, my own stepmother-to-be suddenly Nora, Joan of Lorraine, Catherine of Aragon, Hedda Gabler, yet still somehow herself, her long red hair and the purple shawl she wore during one scene wonderfully familiar to me. I knew that hair was her own, but not attached to her head, cut off when she was young and preserved in a thick braid, kept for future costume needs in a neat plastic wrap in the brightly lit closet she would create for herself out of what was once our dark and boring pantry. I had attached that red hair to my own suddenly dull brown for many a scene in her small apartment a few blocks from our own, played a princess, a witch, an ordinary girl in love—the thick red braid pulled over my shoulder or wound into a crown around my flattened, carefully parted hair. And I wore that long and luscious shawl myself one Halloween, walking the streets of Greenwich Village with my UNICEF jar, trick-or-treating for contributions to save the children of the world.

Yet it was my sister who became a painter, my son an actor. Even then, amid all this enticing possibility, I think it was words that caught me most firmly in their grip.

(But I may be wrong. In part, this is a story about how wrong we can be about so many things. So perhaps it was acting after all, but I was too shy to try. Or, more likely, it was painting and sculpture, which I still love, but I wasn't good enough, or so one revered early teacher thought, and that is when I stopped. Perhaps it was only that I wrote an essay on *Middlemarch* in college and the professor called it brilliant. I set the curve with my A. Which brings me back to my father, the power in his voice and his words, even during his most powerless days.)

Certain words seemed so thick with meaning I could spend a lifetime digging through their layers, like mixing colors on the glass palette to find the perfect shade of green. Words and stories gave me solace. Sentences containing unknown vocabulary or extended lists of adjectives—each one suggested, like the numerous shades of blue, some new specificity. *Dignified* was no mere word but a value, a commandment; nouns, collective and individual, connoted much more than their explicit meaning: *the Working Class*, *Comrade*, the color red and its scintillating plural, *Reds*. The children came to know the communist vocabulary, and it remains in our language today—ironic and humorous at times, at other times perfectly useful, specifically right. For, as in any other discipline, phrases and single words formed us and told us who we were.

When he was putting us to sleep, my father never said, "Good night, comrades." He would never have said such a thing. He would say, "Good night, sw/veet-hearts"—the *v* and *w* as always combined yet distinct in a way that is impossible for me to write on the page. Or he would simply say, "Good night, girls. Sleep well and have pleasant dreams." But I would sometimes change his name for us to that other word he used with the people around dinner tables, in discussions with friends or at political meetings: "Good night, comrades. Sleep well," I'd whisper, pretending he'd used that holy, heroic word. *Comrades.* Not merely friends, not just companions, not only a wife, but sharers in a vision so powerful it had been more sacred than even life itself. For a child already obsessed with the idea of death, its ultimate power and awesome mystery, already in search of the absolute, the very thing itself finally and completely known, and obsessed with a passion it would take me decades to bring down to size and balance, the gorgeous sanctity of this single word could not help but enflame both intellect and imagination. What did it mean, really? What was its history, what inescapable and precious burden had been discovered in its usage and its sound? No simple synonym for anything, you would need a book—hundreds of pages—to exhaust its metaphoric possibilities.

※

Or so I believed until 1958, when my father, George, and others resigned their leadership positions or left the Party completely, a chapter in this story yet to come. Perhaps their losses were mitigated by that particular relief when illusions sustained with much effort are finally dispelled, and reality, however painful or frightening, is faced at last. We were told in solemn tones how Khrushchev had acknowledged in a public speech, then in a more damning secret speech, the murders and mass killings that had taken place in the Soviet Union under Stalin, who I had often heard referred to as Uncle Joe. The break was sudden and unexpected for us, the children. Our parents' actions seemed inexplicable. Suspicions and accusations that for years had formed a kind of background buzz of lies for me had become world-altering truths, and I remember shouting at my father in confusion and anger, denouncing him for his denunciations. Doubts harbored for decades despite stated certainties and true loyalty, once confirmed, may have felt remedial if painful to the adults. Reading all the conflicting interpretations of that period and those people, so many of whom I loved or admired, I hope so. But the breakdown of the Party that had nurtured Bill, had brought him up in a way, that had—in the searing words of one FBI agent—"kicked him around" was a betrayal that brought him to public tears.

CHAPTER 13

FROM FEDERAL BUREAU OF INVESTIGATION,
FREEDOM OF INFORMATION AND PRIVACY ACTS VOLUMES
PERTAINING TO SUBJECT: WILLIAM LAZARRE
FILE NUMBER: 100-1751, SECTION 2

A list of my father's names as it appears in one volume of the voluminous FBI file I obtained through the Freedom of Information Act (FOIA) after some years of effort:

> *Lazar, William* (name on citizenship papers)
> *William (Bill) Lawrence* (his Party name)
> *William Lazzare* (never spelled this way to my knowledge, though
>   when my mother added the "re" to Lazarre, my father changed the
>   more conventional Lazar too)
> *Israel Lazarovitz* (his birth name)
> *I. Lazar* (for Isaac or Israel?)
> *Israel Lazar*

The agents describe him as being **in a fog** since his wife's death, and they are aware as well of his other sorrows: **Bill Lawrence was kicked around by the Robert Thompson clique,** the report states, and this was the beginning of the

FBI's effort to recruit him as an informant. At the Party congress, the report continues, perhaps hopefully, **the attack by Thompson and others, including the accusation of cowardice in Spain, was so brutal he broke down and cried.** This was their chance, they clearly felt, to recruit an important informer, and they began to accumulate and record knowledge of his current life: **Through information received from Confidential Informant (redacted) ascertained on February 7, 1952, that the subject was presently operating a business known as the Merit Cleaners, 325 1/2 Amsterdam Avenue, New York City, with (redacted) of Bell Boulevard, Bayside, Long Island. Subject . . . spends the majority of his time at the aforementioned shop, which caters to the clothes cleaning needs of the area adjacent.**

Merit Cleaners was a small store owned by—who? I have no idea, only that my father's best friend and comrade from Spain, Eddie Bender, who is the unidentified person residing in Bayside, Queens, worked there as a spotter. Where he picked up this ability after all his years in the CP I also don't know, except that, like many others, including Bill, Bender, as we always called him, may have learned the skill as a young immigrant, starting out as a delivery man perhaps—like some of the Asian and Latino men who now deliver my neighborhood's cleaning, some rising to counter and managerial positions—slowly learning the more lucrative skills of the business.

Bill worked the counter, making use of his capacity for polite, witty, often flirtatious (if a good-looking woman was involved) banter, all of which he carried on with his usual mix of erudite formal syntax and the Yiddish/Russian accent with its Slavic musical lilt. He worked at the cleaning store on the Upper West Side of Manhattan for several years following months of withdrawal during a long period of unemployment. He had gone through the money my mother had left him to supplement the small amount paid to him by the Party in his new, lesser posts, but his primary concern and commitment had become fatherhood. Perhaps he was repairing the injuries of paternity he had suffered at the hands of his own violent father. Perhaps his "brokenness"—the word used by friends who wrote about the period, by informants to the FBI, their names redacted in heavy strokes of black, and by the agents themselves—was soothed, however minimally, by retreat to his home. By 1952, a year after my mother's death, the apartment was growing shabby with lack of care and direction, but it still contained large, comfortable easy chairs, pretty flowered wall paper in the kitchen and living room—delicate green leafy vines climbing from floor to ceiling, calming and lovely, though the white background grew grayish-tan as years went by—and included our room, mine and my sister's. Our light blue walls surrounded two large windows that looked out on a quiet backyard and garden. There, on two stone benches facing each other, I had sat with my mother as she rocked the carriage of our new baby, my little sister, then a few years later with my father as we talked about books and commiserated about our loss. Or maybe he was soothed simply by his evening return to us, his children who needed him with the complete and unconditional love of small children no matter, it often seems, the faults or even cruelties of the parents. He folded himself into this love, ours for him, his for us, and during years of depression, though they included some involvement with several women and eventually his marriage, we were, whatever his failures, criticisms or indulgences, the center of his life.

March 10, 1952, evening, about 9 o'clock, PM:

Leaving Merit Cleaners after closing to head home after a long day:

Agents [names redacted] approached William Lazarre on the street at 73rd Street and Broadway. After the agents identified themselves to LAZARRE he cordially greeted them with a handshake and readily agreed to converse with the agents. LAZARRE declined to be interviewed in the Bureau car and, therefore, an agreement was reached whereby the interview took place while the three men were seated on a park bench at 73rd Street and Broadway in New York City. Immediately after the introduction, LAZARRE asked the agents if he were under arrest. He was advised that he was not under arrest. At the outset of the interview LAZARRE was extremely nervous and fidgety and during the entire interview, smoked continuously.

LAZARRE was asked if he had any information concerning the whereabouts of the CP fugitives . . .

[They may be referring to Robert Thompson, Gil Green, Henry Winston, and Gus Hall, who had "jumped bail" rather than be tried for "conspiring to teach, advocate and conspire to overthrow the American government by force and violence."]

Much later, in 1965, in my first college class in political science, the professor—apparently a left-wing progressive, and married, he told us, to a Japanese American woman whose family had been imprisoned during World

War Two, who had since made his subspecialty the Supreme Court decisions that limited or betrayed democracy—shouted at us one afternoon in the sunlit classroom of the then South Campus of City College. "'Conspiring to advocate! Conspiring to advocate!' Do you understand what that means? It has become a crime to THINK. Not only to teach and advocate and plan, but to conspire. To gather with others to talk and THINK. Now YOU think!" he shouted, directing us to write our opinions for homework, pointing at us as we raised our heads from our notes in response to his fervency and passion. "*CONSPIRE.*"

That evening on the Upper West Side:

> **[LAZARRE] made a remark that it was his opinion that perhaps they may know the location of these fugitives and would arrest them at the appropriate time. . . . He stated that no doubt the FBI was well aware of his CP activity. LAZARRE stated he was not ashamed of his past activity since he considered himself a loyal American who did a great deal for the United States Government during World War II. . . . LAZARRE stated that he could not discuss his connection with the CP and stated that he would not make any comments concerning his present connection with the CP . . . that the government could not in any way influence him to reveal or discuss CP activity. . . . At one phase of the interview, LAZARRE clearly stated that even if he had some information of value concerning the CP fugitives or activity he more than likely would not make this information available to the government since he could never bring himself around to the position of informing on the CP or its members.**

Forty years later, at some point in the 1990s, after many years of trying through letters and phone calls, I finally located a woman agent who seemed to want to aid me in securing my legal right to obtain my father's FBI file under the Freedom of Information Act. We became friendly over the course of weekly calls in which I would ask if there had been any progress and she would report, with humorous asides and sincere-sounding apologies, that she was still trying, but there was a lot of "red tape," documents to "go over." Then one day—I remember it as being in early spring; the windows are opened as I picture myself sitting in my study chair—a warm breeze blowing in—or perhaps, unable to divorce myself from a lifetime of making up stories that connect atmosphere and mood, I am making it spring, the warm breeze, the light, because I am so excited and pleased to hear that she is calling me to report success. She has the file. Much has been redacted, she warns, but there is also a great deal (she sighs) of information intact. Where should she send it? I believe from the accents and tones of her voice that she was African American, and here again it may be imagination more than memory, wish locked into the center of an experience as wish is so often buried in a dream, but I do recall with certainty that I had become attached to the familiar lilts of her voice, and in spite of being relieved by her news, I was sorry to lose her on the other end of my phone line. I gave her my address immediately. Since then I have been in possession of a large cardboard box containing many volumes of files, each tome clipped with a long silver wire closure, each with a cover title, "Freedom of Information and Privacy Acts," followed by my father's most commonly used American name, William Lazarre, a file number, and beneath this information a large "Department of Justice, Federal Bureau of Information" seal.

It is a strange and startling record, including narratives, in the old sense of that now-overused word, for threaded through the typical language of bureaucratic memoranda are descriptions that read like stories, of his emigration to this country, character sketches and portraits of my family—my mother, grandmother, sister, myself—and of his brother Isaac, Uncle Buck, Buck Lazar, Itzaak Lazarre to the FBI, Itzaak Lazarovitch to the American immigration authorities and to his old-country family. Some of this information is correct and contains odd pieces of detail: our home phone number; my mother's salary and position at Macy's, where she worked as a buyer in the handbag department; the way she dressed, the color of her hair. Their odd impressions of our family:

> It should be noted that LAZARRE was living a rather gentlemanly life, apparently having money available at any time, it was decided through investigation that his wife, Tullah Deitz Lazarre, was apparently the main support of the family, who made an annual income of approximately $5,000 to $7,000. [considered a large income at the time, in the late 1940s.]
>
> . . . TULLAH DEITZ made an outstanding personal appearance, was considered charming and personable, attractive and intelligent . . . never discussed her domestic life, nor even discussed her husband's position or character. Inquiries show . . . [she] mentioned her husband WILLIAM LAZAR, as being a writer, without further explanation.

After noting my mother's early death, and quoting many of her coworkers referring to her as a "real American" (loyal, but also not an immigrant, I presume), she is further described as (again) **a well dressed, intelligent woman who gave the impression that she was in social standing and intelligence above her husband.**

I remember my mother as "always being well dressed." She was invariably described by friends and family as "elegant," and my father as well as others thoroughly mystified this quality after her death, especially when I donned torn black tights and black sweaters every morning as I grew into a "bohemian" teenager. And while I have no desire to disparage my mother's intelligence, I can be certain that it did not rise above my father's whose capacity for languages, rhetoric, analysis, and memorization was noted even by the judges who sentenced him to prison, the representatives of the House Un-American Activities Committee who questioned him, and by my own memories of his general capacity—an inspiration as well as a hardship at times—to dominate arguments on many subjects with any group or individual with the time and inclination to attend.

>‹

As I read and reread this file, I see that some of the information is correct, containing those odd details, and some of it includes small mistakes. Our home phone number changes over time, though it remained the same for all the years we lived at Greenwich Avenue. My name is given at times as "Jeanne"—and I am described as the younger sister when in fact I am the older. Other mistakes are large and hilariously wrong. For several volumes of hundreds of pages the agents believe there is only one LAZARRE, sometimes calling himself William, sometimes Isaac, one of his many pseudonyms in their opinion, sometimes living in Manhattan on Greenwich Avenue, sometimes in Brooklyn (where my uncle actually lived). Then, many pages, reports, and interviews later, they realize their mistake:

It is to be noted that a Security Index card on Isaac Lazarovitz was maintained in the New York Field Division dated January 9, 1945 . . . on the mistaken premise that Isaac Lazarovitz was also William Lazar, alias Israel William Lazarovitz, William Lawrence, et al. The fact that these individuals were brothers was not ascertained until May 1944. [They had been active and leading members of

the CP since the late 1920s.] The Bureau's attention was then called to this situation by a letter . . . correction is now being made.

The discrepancy in dates may have been due to bureaucratic inefficiency or some other reason. But following the correction, once again the list of my father's supposed aliases appears:

Lazar, William
William Lawrence
William Lazzare
Israel William Lazarovitz
I Lazar
Israel Lazar

At first, the agents clearly mistook Bill's old world graciousness, extended even to them, combined with his always strategic thinking about everything—except for matters in what I soon came to call, teasing him, "the emotional region"—as a sign of his potential as a recruit, an informer on his former and current comrades. Strangely and sadly, he may have contributed to this idea—as he was constantly fighting emotional breakdown during this time—with personal remarks one might make to a possible friend. **"Since my arrival to this country,"** he tells them at one point, **"my life has been filled with personal tragedies. My parents died shortly after we arrived, then a brother, David, in Philadelphia, and now my closest brother, Buck, and my wife."**

Then, back to his more formal vein, **"Gentlemen, [a term he used regularly when speaking to other men—sometimes spoken with humor, sometimes with genuine respect, other times clearly mocking] future contacts with me will be useless. My makeup is such that I could never under any circumstances consider or entertain the thought of giving information on the CP to the government."**

And despite a constantly referred to "informant"—the name redacted, of course—repeatedly assuring them that due to his treatment by the "Thompson Foster Clique" now in control of the Party, Bill would be a potential recruit, the agents finally concluded, **LAZARRE cordial and pleasant, respectful to agents, but . . . he is the type of party member who could not be swayed to cooperate. No further contact is contemplated with LAZARRE.**

Nevertheless, it is clear in the hundreds of pages following this was to be far from the last meeting.

I was only eight in the spring of 1952, but I still see his handsome face drawn in pain and anxiety, his strong body thinning to gauntness. Our once-elegant apartment began to grow more and more shabby, cleaned but much going unrepaired—a torn tablecloth used too frequently, rugs scratched and worn in places to threadbare patches, paint jobs needed for years at a time, rayon curtains from my mother's day finally brought down, too dusty to clean, disposed of in the incinerator down the hall. I see the shabbiness and I cringe. I feel his anxiety as I could not have known it then, and as I imagine him making his way home from Merit's, made late by the enforced street corner meeting with the FBI, I hear stories I was never told, yet the words are as clear as if they are recorded on a tape inside my mind. Entangled with my own memories, I hear his thoughts from decades past as no one can hear the thoughts even of the most intimate people in the present, but I rush to get them onto the page.

The FBI stalks him and what comrades he has left who can still be called comrades. They remind him of the Cossacks, just dressed differently, the Christians in the old country who hated Jews, then, as always, of his own father, with his swinging belt or calloused hand coming down on his sons, the blows his sisters in Philadelphia love to deny. He had run to the hills, leaving his sister Raisela to endure the blows unless Itzaac, the family wanderer, was there to protect her or his mother found the strength to stay her husband's hand. Now he is the only one left to give protection. Itzaac is dead. His father, Nissel, has been replaced by far more dangerous men.

His girls are younger than Raisela—now Rose—was at fourteen, fifteen, shrinking from her father's slaps and insults, and, unlike his sister, his girls have no brother or mother to stand between them and these new, more threatening blows. He pictures, and tries to remove from his mind the pictures of his frightened children. For they must be scared, followed when they are unaccompanied by an adult—to school, to ice cream shops, to their ballet lessons—asked questions about their fathers, learning (too young) to spot (it is so easy) the tall men in beige or black coats, their hair cut short, skin white, expressions harsh or seductive with fake smiles. And worse, answering the door when the men waiting for entrance are clearly agents, children trained to lie—My father is not home, I don't know where he is—given such terrible responsibilities. And himself—he tries to banish that picture too—whether sitting in his room with the door closed if he is home, or out someplace, he is helpless and ashamed. But the shame is nothing compared to the fear. There is talk of Communists being forced to register by the vile McCarran Act sure to be passed soon by the Republican Congress, legalizing deportation on unproven charges of espionage, even for US citizens.

He cannot become a stool pigeon.

He cannot risk arrest, which has happened to many others, or deportation, which was not mentioned but is clearly in their minds. Can they do this to an American citizen? He doesn't know, will have to find out. He lights a cigarette for the few puffs he can ingest before getting on the train.

Where is the solution?

Working behind the counter at Merit's, Bender in the back eliminating stains and spots on dresses and suits, curtains and tablecloths—at times he can momentarily forget. But at night, when he leaves the store for home, especially on this night, the terror returns. My makeup is such that I could never under any circumstances . . . no, he cannot. He will not. He taps the banisters in rhythm as he descends into the subway platform. All the way downtown he longs for another cigarette, fingers his package of Luckies, a few left for the night. He has no idea if threats will materialize, if his citizenship will be revoked, if he will be arrested, if they will try again. He walks quickly the two blocks from the subway to Greenwich Avenue, racing to reach the only home he has ever felt as home since his earliest childhood—despite the dangers, the deaths, the vision of Tullah dying filling every room. Despite Liddy, the greedy landlord always threatening—illegally—to raise the rent so he will have to move. Despite Nash, the hateful super and his equally hateful wife, reading the sensationalist press, frightening the children with threats of police and prison. He has confronted them time and time again, warning them in his most threatening tones, but they continue, each time they find the kids alone. Despite the threat of horrific Christian orphanages made by his wife's ignorant, frightened mother who lived for years with them because none of her other children would take her in. That threat he had discovered just in time to get rid of the old lady, sent her to her daughter, or to her sister, he hadn't cared, one of them had to take her in—the daughter who hated her own mother for some unknown infraction of long ago, the sister whose apartment and life had no extra room.

He walks through the lobby, past the red leather chairs no one ever sits in, each one on the side of a black wrought iron table, its pretty brass lamp and red lampshade suggesting a comfortable, welcoming building that except for a few kind neighbors does not in reality exist. He walks up the single flight of stairs to the second floor, in no mood to wait for the nearly always broken elevator, down the hallway to the north end, apartment 2D, and then, at last, inside.

Rose, this new American Rose, this Negro Raisela, her name the same as his ruined angry sister, is sitting at the kitchen table reading the Daily News, smoking, drinking a tall glass of water.

><

(Many years later, I will read her described in the FBI file as "a Negress maid employed by Lazar whom he pays $50 a week.")

><

Everything is in order, everything is clean. The lights are low, only a small lamp on the table giving her enough light to read. The girls are asleep. Peace seems almost possible. Despite everything, peace for a moment, maybe for an hour, at least until he can get into his bed, close his eyes, kidding himself that maybe tonight sleep will come easily, as it almost never has throughout his entire life. Still, for a moment, peace. The sneers cast as smiles on the faces of the agents begin to fade, behind them his father's face twisted into some incomprehensible rage at his sons and one daughter (never the eldest, never the youngest, always the middle one, Raisela, incurring his wrath)—and now the new Party dictators, "overgrown adolescents" he calls them, their rigid ideologies that will destroy the movement in the end, their cruel accusations—"a coward in Spain." He orders all this to fade, he will focus on the comrades he still loves, the International Brigaders, the Lincolns from America, the wonderful Irishmen, always ready for a drink and a song, used to battling tyrants and ready to risk their lives, the Garibaldi comrades, the Brits, and most of all the Spanish people themselves. His loyal friends, almost brothers, Steve and Bender, now George again, still alive and kicking. He will try to summon them as sentries into his exhausted brain.

He gives Rose a ten-dollar bill, more than enough for a taxi home to Harlem, in addition to the extra pay for staying all evening. She resists, but he pushes it gently into her apron pocket. Soon, she goes to change into her street clothes, put on her makeup, applied no matter what time of night she leaves their house for her apartment uptown, though why she puts on the glistening powder and purple lipstick just to go home to bed he never knows.

I wish I had someone to love me
someone to call me their own
I wish I had someone to sleep with
I'm tired of sleeping alone.
If I had the wings of an angel
Through these prison bars I would fly . . .

He hums the song learned long ago in the Philadelphia prison he still sings while pacing the dark kitchen to quiet his nerves with feelings spoken out loud—the words play silently in his head as he waits for Rose to depart. They share a kind of closeness—she had been with him every day, often every night, when Tullah was dying, and he has no idea how he would cope with anything, with the children, the care they need, without her. Yet despite all this, he has rarely visited her home, once or twice at the most. They never approach anything like socializing together. Despite some common experiences of poverty and lack of formal education, despite the fact—his belief—that in some way they love each other, race divides them. He is her employer, and although she has succumbed finally to his insistence that she call him Bill, that she sit down at the table and eat with them, when he repeats that she is a member of the family, "I work for you," she reminds him gently, but then she pats his arm and even briefly strokes his head, acknowledging her love. Another large source of ignorance in the Party, he realizes, though they have addressed "the Negro question," fought throughout the country for equal rights. Yet their ignorance is obviously vast, and their Negro comrades do not enlighten them—at least he has never been truly enlightened. Still, he has no doubt that tightly woven into his gratitude to Rose is love. Perhaps someone waits for her in her apartment uptown, the reason for the late-night makeup, her musician friend, Russell, who has come to pick her up some nights. Lucky man. Lucky woman.

He sees her emerge from the bathroom in her blue rayon dress. She puts on her old black wool coat, worn in spots but fitting nicely over her long thin body, *cinched at the waist, a dark blue felt hat pulled over her dark hair. "I've laid out the school clothes for the girls," she assures him, and she leaves him with a careful kiss on the cheek.*

><

And then, for a moment, as he turns the locks and leans his forehead against the door, as I often saw him do—behind all the images, the FBI agents threatening, the Party hypocrites accusing, his father's blows, Buck's cold white face, his wife dying—behind them all he may be seeing the hills of Kishinev, and he is running there to get out of the house, through the dark streets toward the hills, where he will sit and look over the city with its scattered lights, the Jewish shtetl to the east, the large Christian neighborhoods straight ahead, the trees, the dark quiet surrounding him.

><

He checks on his daughters, lies down on what had been his mother-in-law's bed, thinking he must move it one of these days, give the girls the extra space for toys and books, for their art table—he will get it out of here this coming weekend, and he imagines himself lugging it somehow into the basement storage room as he drifts off to a sleep of relief—to be here with the children, no Cossacks at the door, his father dead and buried in Philadelphia with Mama, Tullah, and Buck lying next to each other in that enormous Long Island cemetery— but no, don't begin to count the dead, be careful of the unending rivers of grief overflowing banks—mud slipping, slipping—he knows the sorrows locked down in the oldest part of himself, how they can pour in as if the Kishinev hills were striped with rivers, flooding the ground where he sits, flooding his mind, and for once, this night, he heeds his own warnings—don't think of it—you are home—for tonight it will be okay—the words drift in and out as he falls into a dreamless sleep.

CHAPTER 14

His voice again, as if he is in the room with me. The sound is there, the familiar tones and cadences, even the words that can only be inside my own mind, another one of those bridges to him.

Recently I heard the Israeli writer David Grossman talk about his work, the completion of *Falling Out of Time*, a book about the loss of his son in war, a work that includes memories, imagined scenes, poetry, a play. When a writer sits down to begin a new work, he said—in words close to these—he is not only wanting to tell a story, he is deciding what will be the nature of his life for the next two, three, maybe five years. And listening to this wise and honest writer, I thought, yes, that is my desire but also my resistance: Do I really want to continue this resurrection of my father? Do I want to bring him out of the comfort of loss absorbed, to fall out of time? Do I want to feel the old pain slicing through the healing of years of life without him?

But I cannot silence his voice, as if he is reminding me one of the stories I am not eager to remember once again.

>+<

It was when she finally died that I knew I was headed for a breakdown I could not allow myself to have—a breakdown not from the death itself—at least not at first—there was a relief to it, the end of the pain, no hope at all, hoping that like Buck, like Mama, she was at least at peace. I kissed her emaciated face, almost skeletal by then, ran my lips over her skin, now dry and yellowed, hard to the touch. She was gone. The girls motherless, only me between them and destitution. And what did I have? The Party had turned against me. Browder was expelled. I had to fight what I knew was coming, the breakdown from all of it together and, at the same time, I had somehow to find the courage to fight against it while going through it—like the feeling I had at times in Spain—at or near the front, as if a fascist was running toward me, his German rifle pointed at my pathetic ancient gun, my skinny, bony chest, my mind could break into pieces—now afraid of breaking into pieces again though in the relative safety of my own home. My legs felt paralyzed. I fell on my hands and knees. Someplace in the front closet was the cane she had used in her last months of partial mobility, when she could still come out of her room, join us for an hour or so in the living room, sit with us near the Christmas tree—the tree my parents would have cursed, that would have made them faint maybe in disgust and disbelief, but for us, a symbol of internationalism, the unity of all people, and at the same time that we, all of us, Communists and capitalists alike, were Americans, like her, like my wife, a real American. She would lean on that cane and limp into the living room. We would tell the girls, "Mommy had a fall, she will be all right," and then they would open their presents. Now my older daughter cries every night since the death, her screams fill the apartment, these closely connected rooms, one opening into another with only two small hallways in between, her screams begin as soon as the lights are turned out. "I hate you!" She shouts this at me over and over, and, for some unknown reason, "You want me to die!" she cries, sobbing now. "What are you talking about?" I scream back at her—at this desperate child who has always been difficult for me, but as I scream I hold her. She is standing on her bed, her arms clutching my neck as if to protect me from her own words, her tears wetting my neck and the collar of my shirt. "Lower your voice, I plead, you will wake up your sister," though my little one is probably wide awake, listening to the chaos that now reigns. "Count to ten," I plead, hoping the counting might force her to pause in her yelling. "I hate you!" she is screaming. "I wish you were dead instead of Mommy!" I heard this almost every night for weeks after the funeral, since it was all finally over yet not over, never over. And shamefully, but honestly, I allowed myself to whisper to my child, "So do I, ketzeleh, so do I."

Later, when she has finally calmed down enough to sleep maybe for a few hours before she wakes again, screaming again, rushing into my bed to clutch me again, I crawl to the closet, thinking of my wife's courage when her legs were so thin they could hardly hold her up. Someplace it is here—I put it here months ago, and on my knees I touch the dark wood and with the help of the shelf on the closet door I pull myself up. It's there, in the back, and I walk out of the closet leaning on her cane.

CHAPTER 15

What *would* his children do if he were arrested or deported? If his depression had won, defeating the part of his character that overcame and survived? What indeed would we have done? He was our home, for all its encroaching shabbiness, ringing with his own sorrowful nightly songs, he was our security, he persevered, making a valiant effort to keep up family rituals involving food and the demands for collective work. Every Sunday night, when Rose was off for the weekend, he would make dinner, and for special treats we would all walk to the corner store for malted milks to accompany the boiled chicken or broiled lamb chops he cooked. Mine was always vanilla, my sister's chocolate, and I think my father's was strawberry. Every Saturday, again in the absence of Rose's care or in order to "earn" an occasional dinner out at the local Howard Johnsons, we were instructed to thoroughly clean our room, including removing all our books from their shelves so both bindings and shelves could be dusted. After an allotted time, he would come in for inspection, and if the bookshelves remained dusty due to our intentional "forgetting," he would write into the dust with his finger, "Please clean me." At some point a close friend slept over and recruited to help with the cleaning chore expressed her amazement that we emptied and cleaned our bookshelves every single week, and I realized this was not a common practice but my father's personal pedagogy. Now I understand he was trying to keep us all intact, ordering and cleaning what he could so as to push away for a moment all that he could not, just as I do now with my rooms when my life swims into emotional chaos, straightening surfaces, washing clothes, clearing closets, even writing books.

For me, he was everything—teacher, supporter, mother and father, in many ways the more present and therefore primary parent even when my mother was alive and well. Like many in our family and circle of friends, if their stories are to be believed, I adored her, but it was my father who sustained us. I have long known this to be true. Through years of retellings, re/ordering of facts and feelings, apparent comprehension shredded and torn apart again and again, through years of love yet also anger so solid it seemed it might remain petrified forever, through the blessing of his two years as grandfather to my child and the reconciliation that came with that time—through it all, his being occupied a space so large I could hardly step outside of it. And now, after a long retreat into shadows, he is large again.

⋈

We are sitting across from each other in the old kitchen, in the apartment where I spent my childhood, where my mother died years before and where he would die a few years hence. My sister has followed her new love to Berkeley, California. Douglas is in New Haven in the midst of his semester. For the few days I am in New York, we are alone, except for my baby, who sleeps in the other room.

The green linoleum floor has long since been replaced with white vinyl tile, but in my memory I still see it as green. The large table is covered with its black-and-white-checked lined plastic table cloth, tiny tears slowly expanding into full-fledged rips, one large hole covered by a vase of fake but attractive roses. It is evening, and we are eating a light supper, probably herring on rye bread, or boiled eggs and toast for him, for me peanut butter and jam. I am "confronting" him as I have done many times before. Still in my twenties, I am righteously certain of many things, not least my own cherished complaint. "You never loved me," I say—gently, because I am feeling full of love for him as I utter this cruelty. "You preferred my sister. I never lived up to your expectations—I was not beautiful enough, not smart enough, not elegant like you wanted me to be. Like *her*." I search his face. He is either about to cry or shout some old mild epithet, some ancient familiar criticism: *You have always been so . . . so something . . .* I cannot remember the specific adjectives, but they all amount to an accusation of excess—that I feel, say, am too much. I am not certain now, as I recall this scene in the old kitchen, whether I was hoping for the old accusations or for apologetic tears. He speaks to me in a low voice. "That's not true," he says simply. "That has never been true. Though you have always claimed it. I have always loved you, always, unceasingly, and I always will."

><

His voice is louder now than the voices surrounding me in the café where I sit drinking coffee and writing these words in the leather notebook given to me by my son, the little child my father loved now a grown man with a daughter of his own. It is a tone of voice identical to the one I would use with one of my sons if either should ever accuse me of such an absurdity, and so I am left to imagine easily, with no trouble at all, the pain I must have caused him that afternoon in the kitchen where—as I remember it now—rain beat against the windowpanes in the adjoining living room. The rooms were darkening; no lamp had been turned on. I see his face fall into a terrible resignation, an enervation I feel moving into my own aging body as I write.

And then, as I sat there silently gazing at his face, taking in his words, my baby began to cry. I went into my old bedroom, where he slept in a large crib my father had gotten from someplace, secondhand. I picked him up, smelled his milky, tearful sleep smell, and carried him into the kitchen. My father reached out for him. I placed him in his grandfather's arms.

><

It was 2010 when I began thinking and reading about my father's life and legacy again. It is 1951 again. He has been called up on charges by the Party for who knows what sins or crimes or failures of obedience. In all my research I have not found any specifics, only those poignant words by George: "I met my friend Bill Lawrence. I was appalled by his appearance. I was shaken by his interpretations of the upheaval in the party.... I could picture him in the front row, the butt of harsh criticism, his head bowed, unable or unwilling to defend himself—so my friend Bill had fallen."

For perhaps the tenth time I am reading through hundreds of pages of FBI files, and I read the lines I have read many times before: "Subject looks drawn, ashen. Reports prosecutor brought Lazar (alias Lawrence) to tears. Accused him of treason, cowardice in Spain. Possibility for recruitment, in our judgment, is increased."

In the midst of thousands of pages of dull, repetitive, often mistaken information, suddenly this: *drawn, ashen*. Even the agents marked his despair.

PART V   *The Un-Americans*

It began to seem that one would have to hold in the mind
forever two ideas which seemed to be in opposition. The first
idea was acceptance, the acceptance, totally without rancor,
of life as it is, and men as they are: in the light of this idea, it
goes without saying that injustice is a commonplace. But this
did not mean that one could be complacent, for the second
idea was of equal power: that one must never, in one's own
life, accept these injustices as commonplace but must fight
them with all one's strength.

JAMES BALDWIN, "NOTES OF A NATIVE SON"

Joint Resignation Statement by George Charney, William
Lawrence, George Watt: "We, the undersigned, hereby tender
our resignations as officers of the New York State Committee
of the Communist Party and as members of the State Board.
The outcome of the February meeting leaves us no choice."

APRIL 1958, *PARTY VOICE*

CHAPTER 16

Shortly after his resignation, and a few months before he would be called to testify before the House Committee on Un-American Activities, my father met with "Gibby," the nickname for Isadore Needleman, his attorney.[1] Old friends as well as lawyer and client, they discussed my father's situation regarding threats to himself by the FBI as well as the divisions and ongoing arguments taking place during the reconstitution of the Party. Both lawyer and client were certain their conversation was confidential, but clearly they were easily deceived as the entire meeting was recorded and appears in what looks like a word-for-word transcription in the 1951–1958 volume of the FBI file. I am reading the transcription of that conversation now, and as I read I am struck with both their courage and their naiveté.

I can talk freely? Bill asks.

Yeah, his lawyer answers. Turn the fan on. You won't catch cold. It breaks sound waves. That's why I want it on.

In these days of computer hackings and publicly stolen secrets, internet posts, instant messaging and social media of more types than I can keep up with, it might even be called quaint—their willingness to believe their conversations were safely private—if not for the courage it must have taken to confide in each other at all, the trust in the friendship obvious, the risks contemplated by my father frightening and realistic. With the fan as background promising its false sense of safety, Bill begins to describe in detail his most recent meeting with the FBI, but then Gibby turns the fan off altogether, quipping, "I don't want you to get cold."

So I read on, their exact words, I assume, recorded and transcribed by the agents, the document later sent to Director J. Edgar Hoover, adding to the multiple memos and reports on the life and political actions of William Lawrence. Descriptions of his daily life as well as the possibility of recruiting him as an informer—a quest that would become public during the hearing of the House Committee on Un-American Activities to which shortly he would be summoned to testify—all would continue for some time.

"I was met by three of them," Bill confides. "One of them comes up to me as the representative of the Department of Justice. So he has a brown envelope and he said to me, in this envelope I have testimony that you have been recruiting people for espionage. Would you like to sit down with us for a couple of hours? I said to him, no, if you want to talk to me get a warrant. He says, Why? I said, If you have evidence, all you have to do is get a warrant from the judge and pick me up. He said, we want to give you an opportunity to deny it and that will be discussed with you."

There must have been a pause, a weary sigh—the threats had been made, the option of informing offered many times before, as early as 1949. The McCarran Act was still on the books, deportation still a real threat. Likewise, their knowledge of the facts of his life, though sometimes correct, were at times absurdly wrong, so, seeming unperturbed for the moment, he interrupts himself:

"Oh by the way, when I first came out the first thing out of their mouth was congratulations on your marriage."

He does not seem surprised, nor am I any longer surprised by the Bureau's knowledge of our personal life that was, after all, woven tightly into the fabric of my father's political life. So in this interchange they are correct about this one thing. Sometime in the mid-1950s (their dates may be incorrect here and my memory vague) he'd married Maurine, the red-haired actress in whose apartment my sister and I, our cousins and friends, had performed improvisations, dressed up in her intriguing and beautiful clothes. I had come to love two of his previous lovers (the women he called friends, realizing only much later in life the attachments were romantic, though I often so hoped). Mary—to whom I grew almost as close as the "adopted daughter" she named me; we remained close friends until the end of her life.

Gladys, my art teacher, whom I adored more than loved for I did not really know her; I idealized her looks which reflected my mother's dark hair and broad smile, and her work—heavily layered canvasses depicting faces and interiors, as well as her compliments of my beginning efforts as a painter, her words filling my hunger for approval and praise. There were others too who in reality may never have been anything more than friends, though I did not miss the signs of my father's attractions.

Despite my grandmother's warnings about orphanages and mean Catholic nuns, *finally*, is what I thought, as I stood behind him and Maurine at their small wedding before a Connecticut Justice of the Peace, *a real step-mother*. My father was dressed in his usual navy blue suit, carefully cleaned and pressed. I recall a wide pink hat worn by Maurine, its brim encircled with flowers—but I am not certain—it may have assumed that odd reality that can occur when a description has appeared in fiction written before by me. At any rate, in my mind there is a beautiful wide brimmed pink hat worn by the woman who was about to become my legal stepmother. The emphasis for me was on the second half of that word, and unbothered by the reputation of myriad stepmothers in fairy-tales I had of course read and had read to me, I looked forward with excitement and delight to this extravagant woman now coming to live with us.

Despite her fiery temper and endless battles with my father, which began early and would eventually drive them to divorce, battles which we all came to dread, there were years when I thrived in her presence. She introduced new and exciting foods into our bland and repetitive meals—*coq au vin*, a delicious improvement on the boiled chicken and even the Southern fried variety provided by Rose—and permission to sip wine on special occasions. She redecorated the apartment, and even though some of my mother's belongings and all her interior aesthetics began to disappear, I loved the daring new red bookshelves, the replacement of shabbiness with style in every room. She made mistakes in her zeal to improve us, once decorating my sister's and my room with red and white candy striped wall paper and bright bedcovers when we were away from home, then becoming angry at my loud disapproval and insistence on the return of my old black bedspread and demand for repainting of the walls. She fought with our father relentlessly, accusing him of loving his children more than herself—which I believe was true—and of "spoiling us" with his indulgence, which was untrue. But she berated him too for his frequent criticisms of me, generally for my "sloppy appearance" and "terrible temper," and, most important to me, she fought the designation long ascribed to me of "crazy"—the *too much* of more qualities and behaviors than I could count. Like the other artists of the Cultural Region, she found me to be quite ordinary while also recognizing what gifts I may have had, and I relished this new place she'd insisted on for me—a place of belonging. She and I remained close friends long after their divorce in the 1960s, until her own death at the age of ninety-five. By then, she'd had two more husbands, one an Italian psychoanalyst and one a four-star marine general with whom she lived until his death and who, with her usual flamboyance, she was proud to designate as the "best lover she had ever had."

Her career as an actress would be ruined by her appearance before HUAC, an outcome she blamed on the Party whose advisors convinced her to assert her years of membership, wanting to take advantage of her identity as a "true American," a Methodist born and raised in a small Texas town, unlike the many immigrants and especially Jews who comprised much of the Party membership in New York. "Whatever I am, America made me!" She repeated to us this prepared, publicly reported speech she'd made in her best dramatic tones, returning to the deep southern accent that had been replaced by the unregionalized English she had attained for her theatrical career. At first she was proud as she quoted herself, then furious when she began to realize she would never work again, except in small regional and college theaters. Blacklisted and used, she resigned from the Party, went back to college in her mid-fifties and became deeply involved in the study and eventual teaching of both physical and spiritual disciplines. Douglas and I visited her several times in the home she had shared with the general until his death, where she continued to live until her own death years later. It was a house set deep in a rural town on the western shore of the Chesapeake in Maryland. There, we were included in her morning yoga stretches, introduced to her many followers and friends from the local college and its theater where she had performed, and given numerous books about psychosynthesis, the philosophy of self-awareness and personal transformation to which she had become devoted.

>+<

After his brief reference to his new wife, my father continues his report to Gibby about the agents' attempt at a friendly exchange. "They think they have a trick up somewhere, so I said, suppose you come tomorrow."

He was trying, I suppose, to get rid of them and end the meeting, but not before they referred to some enemy who had once accused Bill of pushing someone (name redacted) out of a window.

Gibby laughs, and Bill continues his description.

"This guy—he wrote a whole story about it. Believe me. Big headlines... That was two years ago . . . but wouldn't the FBI like . . .

(A pause, or perhaps a muffling of some words . . .)

". . . The agent was extremely mild and I was extremely vulgar. I told him, I said, if you fellows think with that line of . . ."

(*bullshit*—clearly the word too obscene for the agent writing the memo—is redacted;)

". . . with that line of . . . you are going to try to frighten me or intimidate me go ahead and do it. Well, we were standing there, you see, three of them surrounding me. I mean I was in a semicircle. But after I would say, seven or eight minutes, I broke away. As I left one of them said to me—'Hey, is (redacted name) remaining in the Party?' They always try to get me to become a stool pigeon, but this is the first time they have raised the question of espionage. Now my question is the following: If they have some evidence like that, they wouldn't tip me off, would they? They'd watch me and pick me up?"

"Of that you can be sure," Gibby answers. But my father wants confirmation.

"So, they are just trying it as a method of intimidation, and they think that maybe that I'd get, you know, panicky about the whole thing?"

His lawyer reassures him—the threats are fantasy, pure fiction.

"The Party is breaking up. People will be demoralized. So they are approaching guys. I wouldn't give it another thought. . . . They planted a letter on a client of mine written in Yiddish—it's addressed to my client from his brother, who is on the other side—saying in Yiddish that he is being held in prison."

I read "the other side" to mean the Soviet Union. It was not simple paranoia that led our families to talk in code on the telephone, some of our fathers, uncles and friends to "go underground." People were arrested, deported or sent to prison for speech, for the written word. Many lost their jobs and careers, were barred from their professions. There was a rash of suicides, divorces, people fell suddenly ill with life threatening diseases.

Gibby then returns in detail to the story of the letters planted then "discovered."

"Months later the same brother writes another letter saying he is fine, including photos of himself and his family. And this guy knows his brother's handwriting, and they never write in Yiddish. . . . But he was disturbed by it."

Resuming his legal advice, he then must have changed his tone, asking Bill if he ever had any dealings with (name redacted) in his "cultural activity," . . . perhaps the individual now accused of espionage, used as an entrapment to frighten my father into collaborating.

"Maybe," Bill answers. "I will check."

➤◄

According to the transcript copied from whatever bug was obviously in the room, they then turn to a discussion of the difficulties engulfing the Party, and they speculate about possibly resigning not only leading positions but membership altogether. Bill describes Bob Thompson, by then a powerful leading spokesman, soon to be Executive Secretary of the Party, as an "overgrown kid . . .

I want to tell you," he says, "that Thompson is just as wicked on one side as (name redacted) is on the other. Neither of them has a creative idea or even a thought. He—(referring it seems to Thompson)—ruined the Transport Workers Union."

This allusion involves an argument about what the Party's role should be in a union demand that the five-cent subway fare be increased. For some reason, I suppose the old battle between aligning with labor movements and other progressive organizations versus keeping apart from internal capitalist fights, Thompson objected to any support for the union and warned that anyone who spoke up for it would be "characterized as a traitor and a turncoat."

"Lazar became angry," the FBI agent writes, "and threatened to resign then and there. He believed Thompson and other leaders of the Party had people 'terror stricken.'"

"Where is the dignity," my father asks about someone who had been attacked by the new Party Elite. "Where is the self-respect?"

As the discussion continues, he is quoted again: "He can't ride me out of the Party the way he tried in '45. I'm going to oppose his behavior."

They talk further in this vein—the increasing polarizations, threats and entrenched views within the Party as well as of the "highly placed informants" referred to as "needing protection" in the FBI report.

><

Although I am reading the content of this meeting twice removed, and the transcript is in the file compiled by the FBI, it is one of the sections that rings true to me. My father's views and syntax are familiar. I can hear the anger and disgust, the analytic and decisive tone.

In March of 1958, when Bill resigns from the New York State staff as treasurer and membership director of the New York District, he declares it is the first time he has ever resigned a post despite disagreements, but he would retain his membership, and as far as I know he did so until he died.

The file ends in June 1958, with these words:

"Subject subpoenaed Saturday 7:00 AM for appearance before HUAC, Executive Session on 6/17/58 in NYC. Lazar intends to invoke 5th Amendment on all questions except those referring to Lazar's name, address, occupation and education. He also states he knows they are going to ask him and accuse him of sentencing Americans to death while Commissar in Spain, and he characterizes this as 'a contemptible lie.'"

CHAPTER 17

JUNE 1958

It is a late spring day, warm, up in the high 80s he thinks, prediction for 90. He loosens his tie, unbuttons his shirt collar. It's been dry for weeks, and he wishes for a sudden rain as he makes his way up the steps of the Courthouse on Foley Square in New York City. He is not intimidated, only prepared. He has no more to fear from these guys, he hopes, than from his old dead father. There is nothing they can do to him now, though he suspects they will try again. Still, the threat of deportation that he has been assured is extinguished remains—others have been deported; proof is not always needed. But he has weathered the fear of death in Spain and here he is, over twenty years later, alive, bloodied but unbowed, as one poet said, one of his favorites, though he can't remember which one. He has survived the death of his young wife, leaving him with two little girls to mother and father at once, and it seems—people say—he thinks so—he hasn't done a bad job so far. One is almost an adolescent, the other already in those reportedly notorious years. In the old country by the time you were thirteen you were a man or a woman. His sisters were cleaning and cooking all day. Long since out of school, he'd gone to work in his father's teahouse and joined the local Communists, begun his Marxist education. He doesn't believe there is even a word for adolescence in his old language, or at least he doesn't know it. His older daughter is a handful, lots of fights and temper tantrums. But she is

smart and has her mother's face, even if she does not dress carefully, even if he
wishes she would be more interested in her appearance, like the woman she looks
so much like. And his little one—vulnerable and often frightened, but no real
problem with her. Her blond hair and blue eyes remind him of his own family.
Her skin, even approaching those rough teenage years, shines pink and gold.
She cries a lot—sensitive, maybe too sensitive—but both of them are okay.
Both talented at painting, he is told, so artists*—he thinks the word with a mix*
of pride and concern. He wants them to be independent, to have the means of
earning a living—teachers, maybe even lawyers—that's what he wants for
them. And now they have a new mother, a woman to influence them—though
she is an actress, always overdramatic—but no, he is sure, they will be okay.

The self-satisfied, arrogant men are gathering. The lights are almost blinding.
Photographers are everywhere—he will have to object to that. Moulder, that
son of a bitch, is calling the committee to order. He is called. He knows what he
has to do. He clenches his fists. He is ready for a fight.

TESTIMONY OF WILLIAM LAZAR (WILLIAM LAWRENCE)
ACCOMPANIED BY COUNSEL, ISADORE G. NEEDLEMAN[1]

Mr. Lawrence, kindly come forward.

So. Already it starts. Gibby answers for him.

I represent Mr. Lazar. Possibly you mean him. If you are calling Mr. Lazar, I represent him.

Lawrence. They want his party name, for obvious reasons. As if he is a nincompoop.

Does my client have to walk into this barrage of photographers?

Arens (Staff Director): Mr. Lazar, will you kindly come forward, pursuant to the subpoena?

Attorney Needleman: He is in the courtroom and when the photographers sit down, he will come forward.

He is called again. And again. All this is expected, of course, a kind of script, a play to be performed, his own part rehearsed. Now it's his turn:

May I ask the photographers as fellow workmen to please refrain from taking pictures of me? I respectfully request, gentlemen, that you will not take pictures.

Moulder (Representative from Missouri): The Committee will conduct the hearing in accordance with what we believe to be the proper conduct and we are

doing so. We now, of course, respectfully request the photographers to refrain from taking any pictures while the witness is testifying.

Do you solemnly swear—

Arens: Kindly identify yourself by name, residence, and occupation.

So it begins, just like in '47, the writers, some of them his pals from the Cultural Region days. The Hollywood Ten. In '48 Hiss, not even a Communist yet imprisoned for five years for so-called perjury. The Rosenbergs, executed only a few years before as Soviet spies, supposedly giving away atomic secrets—it is still a terrible time, a dangerous time. He'd sat in his small bedroom where he kept his radio, his daughters near him, others too—he can't remember who, how many. But he remembers the somber silence in the room. Electrocuted, both of them. The endless minutes of waiting. And the announcement that they were dead. They were all quiet, the adults grim, the kids crying, shocked and scared as they listened to the commentator's voice conveying the horrible news. It wasn't all just about lying to the FBI then, not just shouting about righteous politics to their friends, not even knowing some of the comrades who had been sent to prison. Killed. Some of the Communist fathers and mothers could be killed.

He had not wept, but he'd looked down at the floor for so long his daughters had come over and put their arms around him. Dalton Trumbo had come to mind, a great writer who has to work under a pseudonym now, who made a movie out of Fast's novel about Spartacus, leader of the Roman slaves. "I am Spartacus," the masses of gladiator-slaves had shouted when the Roman generals demanded the real leader identify himself. No one to stand up now for him—no crowd shouting, "I am Bill Lawrence!" But he doesn't need it. He has no job to lose, no career to ruin, only has to protect himself from indictment so the girls won't be left alone. That is all he has to think about. He has to bring his thoughts back to this hateful room, away from the past.

William Lazar. 30 Greenwich Avenue. Spotter by trade.

After being instructed he is not allowed to smoke, he is invited to make a brief statement.

So you wish . . .

And, Yes, Sir, I do.

All of it so formal, a ritual of deception, as if anger can be put away on his side, vengeance and hypocrisy on theirs.

I would like to challenge the jurisdiction of this committee, first, because I feel it has no legitimate legislative function and, to the best of my knowledge, not a piece of legislation has emerged as a result of the functioning of the so-called Walters committee. . . . The function of this committee, sir, is not yet defined and it is rather vague. I also consider, based on the record of this committee, that in questioning witnesses this committee violates my constitutional rights in probing my personal beliefs, associations, or affiliations. Finally, may I say Mr. Chairman, that it seems to me that this committee is as outmoded and outdated as is the covered wagon, with this difference: The covered wagon helped build a good and beautiful America. Thank you.

It moves forward, to the inevitable.

Mr. Lazar, for the purpose of identification, kindly tell us if you have been known by any name other than the name Lazar.

I shall decline to answer that on the grounds of the First and Fifth Amendments.

Have you been known by the name of William Lawrence?

I shall decline on the grounds of the First and the Fifth Amendments.

Do you honestly apprehend, sir, if you told this committee truthfully while you are under oath whether or not you have been known by the name of William Lawrence you would be supplying information which could be used against you in a criminal proceeding?

Sir, your concept and my concept as to what I apprehend are entirely two different things. I challenged the rights of this committee to probe into my personal affairs.

✦

More interchanges follow on "differences in apprehension of the dangers of incrimination." He is asked for the place of his birth, to which as if by rote he again invokes the First and Fifth Amendments, but then:

Mr. Chairman, on advice of counsel I shall state I was born in the city of Kishinev, Russia.

It is ascertained for the record that Mr. Lazar is a citizen, naturalized in 1926 in Philadelphia, arrived in the US in 1921. Under what name were you naturalized?

The First and Fifth Amendments are invoked once again.

At the time of your naturalization were you a member of the Communist Party?

It has been decided by legal counsels, by the Party, by many who have already appeared before this primitive tribunal, that he will invoke the First and Fifth as many times as they ask him their ridiculous, obvious questions. What do they think? What do they believe? That he is so easily tricked after a life-time of revolutionary discipline and study? He is both furious and exhausted. Sometimes he can't tell the difference. But what he can do is present a calm exterior. "I am the captain of my soul"—another line, maybe from the same poem. He can hide his emotions when necessary, though he feels them strongly, often extremely strongly, too extremely if some of the women he has loved are to be believed, like his daughter—who has yet to learn to control her emotions. "Count to ten," he admonishes her each time she begins to explode, more and more frequently of late, maybe reflecting the tensions all of them feel. "Count to ten!" But she ignores him, slams her door, still shouting. He feels it in his own gut, like the screams are his own.

And now he thinks of Paul Robeson's words, a couple of years before appearing before this same so-called committee, a bunch of legal vigilantes for all he can see. He'd reread the testimony of the great actor and singer the night before, and it all rushes through his mind now, Robeson's heroic statements, his un-compromising rhetoric.[2]

Arens and his committee cohorts had asked about revoking Robeson's passport unless he submitted an affidavit declaring he was not a Communist. Represented and advised by counsel, Leonard Boudin, Robeson replied, "Under no conditions would I think of signing such an affidavit—in a complete contradiction of the rights of American citizens." Asked if he voted for the Communist Party, he responded, "Would you like to come to the ballot box when I vote and take out the ballot and see?" Again and again, he invoked the Fifth: "I invoke the Fifth Amendment and it is none of your business. . . . I invoke the Fifth Amendment. And forget it."

Sitting in the apparently indestructible wingback chair the night before, the house dark except for the one lamp he reads by, he could almost hear the low baritone, the confident delivery: "Wherever I have been in the world—Scandinavia, England, and many places, the first to die in the struggle against fascism were the Communists and I laid many wreaths upon the graves of Communists. . . . And the Fifth Amendment has nothing to do with criminality. The Chief Justice of the Supreme Court has been very clear on that in many speeches. . . . I invoke the Fifth Amendment."

Looking up from the page he had laughed out loud as the idiot Arens tried to bait Robeson: "The witness talks very loudly when he makes a speech but when he invokes the Fifth Amendment I cannot hear him."

But Robeson had shot back, "I invoked the Fifth Amendment very loudly. You know I am an actor and I have medals for diction." *Then he'd managed some sarcastic baiting himself of that son of a bitch Walter.*

"The Pennsylvania Walter?" he asked, obviously pretending politeness.

"That is right."

"Of the coal mining workers and not United States Steel, by any chance?" *Reading the testimony the night before, he could hear the sarcasm as if Robeson were speaking right there in the room.*

"The author of all those bills that are going to keep all kinds of decent people out of the country?"

"No. Only your kind."

"Colored people like myself, from the West Indies—just the Teutonic Anglo-Saxon stock you would let come in."

"When I am abroad I speak out against the injustices against the Negro people of this land."

On and on it went, and he had read it all, sleepless, anticipating his own appearance.

"I belong to the American resistance movement which fights against American imperialism, just as the resistance movement fought against Hitler." *So Robeson still believed. He, too, still believes, though he has come to doubt the Party as the instrument of that faith.*

"Why do you not stay in Russia?"

"Because my father was a slave, and my people died to build this country, and I am going to stay here, and have a part of it just like you. And no fascist minded people will drive me from it. Is that clear?"

Then, as always, skin color prejudice was mockingly denied. "You graduated from Rutgers and you were graduated from the University of Pennsylvania. I remember seeing you play football at Lehigh."

"And we beat Lehigh," *Robeson played along, but then added,* "That is something that I challenge very deeply, and very sincerely, that the success of a few Negroes, including myself or Jackie Robinson can make up—for seven hundred dollars a year for thousands of Negro families in the South. . . . I have cousins who are sharecroppers and cannot read or write. I do not see my success in terms of myself."

He'd finished the document, turned off the light, maybe get a few hours sleep before the hearing. "They lived not for themselves alone." *Once again he sees the words etched into the stone entrance to the plot of graves where Tullah and Buck are buried, side by side.*

⊁⊀

Arens is apparently repeating a question, louder and louder, almost splitting his one good eardrum, cutting into his reverie.

Mr. Lawrence . . .

Lazar is the name.

Do you deny your name is also Lawrence?

A copy of the article from two months earlier is presented, "Three State Reds Resign Posts," and Arens is reading aloud from the article: One is William Lawrence, Treasurer.

And so again:

Mr. Lazar, we want you to tell us, after you look at that article, whether or not you are now, at this moment, a Communist.

A new sort of response, his words coming to him as if he were writing a story, a nice kind of protection even when the story is the god honest truth:

Mr. Chairman, would you permit me to ask counsel just how would it serve our Nation if you knew whether I am or am not a member of the Prohibition Party?

Prohibition Party?

Or any Party.

The chairman provides a short lecture on the distinction of the Communist Party from any other Party—"the Communist operation uses this façade behind which it operates. . ."—followed by more interchanges about the distinctive dangers to the welfare of the United States by the Communist Party/conspiracy/operation.

Arens . . . I respectfully suggest that the witness be ordered and directed to answer that last outstanding question.

It's becoming hard to take them seriously. He glances at Gibby, eyes questioning. Gibby smiles, and he takes the smile as encouragement. Why not annoy them a little? It can't hurt.

You know, Mr. Chairman, this reminds me of a cartoon that appeared in yesterday's New York Post.

That is not in response to the question. The witness is directed to answer the question asked by counsel.

In other words, all you want is the truth as you see it.

Kindly answer the question.

What is the question again, please?

The question is: Are you now, at this moment, a Communist?

I decline to answer on the grounds of the First and Fifth Amendments.

⇥⇤

At this point a new witness, John Lautner, is brought in to identify Bill Lazar ("alias Izrael Lazar"), and he testifies under oath that he is the same as Bill Lawrence, formerly an organizer for the Communist Party.

Lautner: When I first became acquainted with Bill Lawrence he was a section organizer of the Communist Party in New York—Section 10, Queens. . . . This was in the years 1933, 1934, and 1935. I was a section organizer, likewise, in a different section of the party. . . . We used to go to weekly meetings for a number of years together. If my recollection is correct, somewhere around 1935, Bill Lawrence became the section organizer of the Communist Party in the needle trades; and I think he was in that capacity at the time I left New York City.

At that particular time, Bill Lawrence was functioning in the capacity of State Executive Secretary of the Communist Party of New York State under the leadership of Gil Green. He functioned in that capacity, I think, up to 1945. At the emergency convention in 1945, there was a leadership change in New York State, and he left that capacity. I left the party January 17, 1950. After that period Bill Lawrence was drawn back into the State leadership again under the leadership of George Charney Blake—as treasurer—when his resignation appeared in the New York Times.

After a lengthy exchange on the different opinions of Communists with regard to events in the Soviet Union, Arens suspends Lautner's testimony and the witness is excused. My father is listening to a paid informer giving information to which he will eventually be asked to respond, and except when he chooses to engage, he will repeatedly take the Fifth. I picture his hands moving into fists, knuckles rubbed against knuckles—he despises stool pigeons almost as much as he despises fascists—then fingers extended, brought together in a silent clap, and, if there is a surface nearby, the characteristic sign of controlled anxiety, the repeated tapping while he thinks and tries to calm down.

⇥⇤

The testimony of William Lazar resumes:

Arens: Mr. Lawrence, excuse me, Mr. Lazar. You have heard the testimony of Mr. Lautner stating in effect that up until 1950, while he was in the high echelon in the Communist Party, he knew you as a member of the Communist Party. We want to afford you an opportunity now, sir, while you are under oath to deny that testimony. Do you care to avail yourself of that opportunity?

Lazar: I have too much self-respect to debase myself on testimony of informers and paid stoolpigeons.

Scherer (of Ohio): I think Mr. Lautner is a patriotic American and he has rendered a valuable service to the United States — but irrespective of the fact that you think he might be a stoolpigeon . . .

Lazar: I think he might be . . .

Scherer: . . . is he telling the truth about you or is he lying to this committee? I assure you if you say he is lying, I am going to ask that the committee refer both your testimony and his testimony to the Department of Justice, so now you have the opportunity, if this man you called a stoolpigeon. . . .

It comes again—the old repeated threat. That they will revoke his citizenship, deport him, like they did Marty—and who knows where he is now. For a moment it is 1926 again and he is swearing to uphold the Constitution, his hand raised with the others, his wife, her hand raised too, standing next to him—William Lazarovitz—then a couple years later his name legally changed on his papers to William Lazar, the name they are now trying to deny as authentic. Itzrael Lazarovitz, Izrael Lazar, William Lazar, later with Tullah's added re, Bill Lawrence—all of them himself—he banishes the images, forces his attention back to the interrogators, powerful men with the power to ruin his and his children's lives.

I decline to answer the question on the grounds of the First and Fifth Amendments.
I thought you would.

Now Arens again:

Now, sir, kindly tell us what was your last principal employment prior to the employment which you presently have?

After conferring with counsel, Bill responds as usual on the grounds of the First and Fifth.

Arens: How long did this last principal employment which you had endure?
I decline to answer that on the grounds of the First and Fifth Amendments.

We started with your present employment. What was the employment you had prior to this, which we shall call your No.1 employment?

He knows of course what they are after—his résumé, as it is now called, his work history for the Party. From state secretary to section organizer to managing editor of the Worker *to director of the cultural region and others in between—all of his positions, from large to small, from significant to fill-ins because the cowards now leading the Party were perhaps afraid to get rid of him altogether. And now, no position at all, just an ordinary membership—a bit more solid than all the "fellow travelers" as they call themselves, the ones who are too scared or rightfully self-protective to join officially but believe in the work, in the ideals and the goals. A bit more than them, but not much more, lately not much more at all. He can only try to confuse his questioners by pretending to confusion of his own, to ward off the threat, still far from neutralized, of deportation, maybe even some trumped-up espionage charge leading to prison.*

Lazar: Counsel, you are getting me slightly confused. You are asking in terms . . . frankly, I don't know what you are talking about.

Arens: You have had employment prior to your present employment, is that correct?

Lazar: Do you mean was I working?

Arens: Yes, sir.

Lazar: Off and on, and when I had a chance to work I worked and when I got tired I got another job.

Arens: Did you work as general manager of the Daily Worker, as Mr. Lautner stated?

Lazar: I decline to answer that on the grounds of the First and Fifth Amendments.

Arens: Were you cultural director or cultural commissioner of the Communist Party?

Lazar: What is that?

Arens: Mr. Chairman, I respectfully suggest that the witness be ordered and directed to answer the question.

Moulder: The witness is directed and ordered to answer the question if he knows.

Lazar: Mr. Chairman, I am sure you expect an intelligent answer. I must comprehend, I must understand the question. I am merely asking counsel for . . .

Moulder: Do I understand you to say that you do not know what cultural director is, or was, in the Communist Party?

Lazar: Yes, I want the counsel to tell me what he is talking about.

Moulder: The question is, do you know what the cultural director was, or is, in the Communist Party?

Lazar: No, I do not know.

Arens: Did you have charge of cultural activities for the Communist Party?

Lazar, after conferring with counsel: I decline to answer on the grounds of the First and Fifth Amendments.

And then the questions shift, from the cultural region days to the Spanish Civil War, his and others' illegal travel into Spain as members of the International Brigades.

Arens: Joseph Klein swore before this committee in April 1954 that he knew you as a political commissar for the International Brigade in the Spanish Civil War. Was he in error on that statement?

The First and Fifth are invoked again.

Arens: Have you ever traveled abroad since you became a citizen of the United States?

Lazar: Same answer, sir, First and Fifth.

Arens: Have you ever applied for a United States passport?

Lazar: I decline to answer on the grounds of the First and Fifth Amendments.

Arens: Do you now have information regarding the use to which members of the Communist conspiracy place passports in the operation of the international conspiracy?

Lazar: I decline to answer on the grounds of the First and Fifth Amendments.

And on to the next attempt at breaking his vows not to inform, not to aid their illegal interrogations in any way at all.

Arens: Can you help this committee by giving us information respecting present Communist activities in the entertainment industry in the New York area by members presently active in the party?

Lazar: Would you please repeat that question?

Arens: Do you have information now, sir, respecting persons known by you to be Communists who are in the entertainment industry?

Lazar: I decline to answer on the grounds of the First and Fifth Amendments.

Arens: Mr. Chairman, I respectfully suggest that we conclude the staff interrogation of this witness. I respectfully suggest now if it meets with the Chairman's approval.

Have they actually concluded, or are they giving up? He is silent, not even a glance at Gibby. He looks straight ahead.

Scherer: I am going to ask that the committee refer the testimony of this witness to the Department of Justice to determine whether or not denaturalization proceedings can be instituted.

Robeson's words come to him again—"You are the Un-Americans, and you ought to be ashamed of yourselves."

Moulder's words intrude:

The witness is excused.

Papers collected, he and Gibby rise to depart. He is concerned, but all in all it wasn't bad, he tells himself, not bad at all.

CHAPTER 18

The Justice Department will not deport him. He will not be sent to prison. In the years to come he will find work in a local restaurant and then a factory—both owned by former comrades. While his daughters attend city colleges that were then completely free, he will read and study while they do the same. One reads novels and poetry, one paints and studies the history of art. He meets old friends, divorces, finds a few other women to spend time with. But no new love claims him. Off and on he feels the old depression threaten; then he forces himself to go out to a movie, attend a lecture. He writes regularly to his congressman, John Lindsay, advising, approving or criticizing his votes. As the civil rights movement gains energy, he reads every article he can find, watches the news on TV every night—dogs attacking young nonviolent activists, white faces filled with hate shouting at school children, lynching rampant again, the right to vote denied after all the years of struggle. When Reverend King is assassinated, he becomes a loyal witness, as up close as he can be. He takes the subway to Harlem, the PATH train to Newark, to see the uprisings, called riots by the capitalist press, with his own eyes. By then it is 1968. His daughter is just married to a man he has recently learned to call black, an African American—Douglas, the son-in-law he has already begun to love.

⊹

Most nights he is alone in the apartment, eating something light for dinner, reading papers and books until it's time for the television news. Plenty of time to think—too much time. Often he is back in Spain, and there is Oliver Law, a heroic son of the black working class, a cement factory worker, a cab driver, a Communist, in Spain a military hero—and whatever the racists and anti-Communists said at the time, Law had earned his position—they all knew that. No matter if the leadership had wanted a black man to command. That was the principle. Law, the individual, had been given what he deserved. The first black American ever to command white soldiers—his words, recounted by someone—never forgotten. We came to wipe out the fascists—he had said, something close to that—some of us must die doing that job—the exact words came back now—but we'll do it here in Spain, maybe stopping fascism in the United States without a great battle there. He grasped Law's meaning even better now than he had then.

And the honor of meeting Langston Hughes, introducing him by a letter to Ed Rolfe, also a commissar, asking him to facilitate introductions and contacts so the great writer could tell the story of the Negro comrades of the 15th Brigade. Help him in whatever way possible—he had written, and he felt proud of it now. It all seemed possible then. It all seemed immanent.

⁜

What remained for him then I still wonder now, for all of them who were resigning posts, giving up membership completely in the Party—the instrument of years of struggle and belief? Hopes for a better world are always grounded in part in personal stories, the individuals one loves, places and habits one keeps alive with cherished significance—so friends gathered, shared meals, and always engaged in political conversations. For some of these men and women, though hearts were broken and minds were near to splitting by Khrushchev's revelations and admissions, hope and even belief somehow remained. Others relinquished all commitment to the Marxist philosophy to which they had harnessed all their dreams for a "just and better world."

Many years later, when most of them had left the Party—which, my father was fond of saying, could no longer fill its meetings in a telephone booth, whereas once they could fill Madison Square Garden—when many of them including my father had died, George's daughter Ruth, still my very close friend, and I asked a few of the women and men who had quit during the late 1950s, who were now aging, living out more ordinary daily lives than they had ever experienced before: What happened? How did you continue to believe? How could you have denied for so long what was really going on in the Soviet Union under Stalin?

"We had so much hope, and it was a very different time," one man said, sitting in his tiny wooden cabin on a hill in Truro, Cape Cod, perhaps searching back through the years in his mind's eye as he stared past us at the unpainted hand built walls.

Hattie, Ruth's mother who survived her husband by many years, a woman I had been close to all my life, responded, "We were wrong about many things, but the times—they were so . . ."

Different, I suppose she might have said—or, filled with lies and liars—or, we had to hold on to the beliefs we had sacrificed everything for—it takes a long, long time to relinquish faith and betray commitment. But none of this was said, and I had never before heard her at a loss for words. Her voice, to me at least, usually came from certainty about everything, never from digging down for language to fit something still protean and obscure. She was known for her harsh discipline, of herself and of others, known for her bravery and courage in a crisis—and she had seen some in her life. "If I were crossing the country in a covered wagon," Douglas is known for repeating after years of knowing her, "I would want Hattie sitting shotgun." But on the day of my question I saw confusion in her expression, as if she were momentarily overwhelmed by an inability to comprehend. Then, eyes clear and a self-mocking turn to her mouth, she recovered her more usual acceptance of reality. We were sitting on a couch in Ruth's Massachusetts home, where we often met, she from Florida, me from New York, for a three-way reunion filled with talk of recent novels read, the lives of her growing crowd of grandchildren. "We were wrong about many things," she said firmly and turned back to Nadine Gordimer's most recent story about the daughter of a Communist father in apartheid South Africa. At a safely renewed distance, we spoke of the widespread injustice there.

꘎

We, the children, moving through our adolescent years, were arrogant at times, for we had been spared much of the agonizing story of splits or, too young to understand, told only the headlines. In my family the entire struggle of the American Communist Party, however central it had been to our father's life, was always overshadowed by the unending sad and mournful atmosphere of our home even years after our mother's death, even during Bill's marriage to Maurine. There were times of joy and pleasure, humor and celebration, but the pall of her loss was never really overcome.

A large portrait hung in our living room. Our mother stared out at us dressed in what looked like a satin cloak of forest green, a stunning pink flower at the center of its slope. Her tan shoulders and face looked strong yet feminine. Her dark hair fit her lovely head like a cap. And her dark eyes were painted so that wherever you walked in the room they appeared to follow you. She watched me. She looked at me as I read, or watched our new television, or just stared back at her. You could not escape.

This painting remained on the living room wall for some time after Maurine had married into our family and begun to redecorate our home. Finally, either out of loyalty to my new stepmother or concern for my father's obvious denseness, I insisted that, for Maurine's sake, he take it down. He did, and I was granted the approval of my father and the gratitude of his wife. But today it seems clear I was acting primarily in my own behalf— getting rid of the thing without having to suffer guilt. For I had sworn—and I was subtly encouraged in this destructive vow by many of the adults who dominated my childhood—my mother's sister and mother, but also my father—that I would somehow never cease thinking about her. So when I did pause in my habitual compulsion, I forced myself to concoct complicated rituals of apology and abject confession made to what I came to call the Invisible Audience, always with me, judging and condemning until I obeyed the rules again. And it was not until I was in my own middle age, mother of two adolescent sons, having written several books in which my mother figured centrally as herself or as a character altered to varying degrees by fiction, always with more books and slightly altered stories taking shape in early notes, not until I had spent hundreds of hours in two different analytic sanctuaries describing, remembering, dreaming, loving and hating her, that I would feel I had completed my sacred requirement and could begin to let her go. Today, after a few more books and one more analytic couch, the most profound and successful of all my interior journeys, I finally think of my mother as herself—a very young woman whose joy of life remains within me through memories of her love songs, her games, her drawings, her gorgeous clothes, and whose tragic, long and painful death must have been even more frightening to her than to her two young daughters, whose lives and whose children's lives, as my older son once put it, would be haunted by her for decades, a long inability to mourn.

⊁⊀

The Party breakup remained a central theme in our lives during the 1950s and into the early 1960s. Mr. and Mrs. Nash, our superintendent and his wife, shouted at us as we entered the lobby, taunted us when we walked out the double doors on our way to school: *Your father is a traitor. Go back to Russia. He's going to prison this time.*

We had been taught to ignore these "ignorant imbeciles," or to face them squarely and tell them to leave us alone. As young children we were empowered by sticking our tongues out at them. But Mr. Nash entered our daily anxieties and our nightly dreams. When we made too much noise, when in some sibling battle one of us, usually me, threw something out the window into the yard below and the bell rang, we knew it was Mr. Nash, probably coming to kill us or at least haul us off to prison with the other Communists, and we ran for the closets, refusing to come out until Rose, our trusted protector, could get rid of him. Still, we were terrified of a trip to the basement to retrieve a bike from the storage room or help gather the clothes from the washing machines down there, fears of Mr. Nash lurking or attacking always present even when we were old enough to know he was essentially harmless. Until I moved out in my twentieth year, when I graduated from City College in 1964, I much preferred the one flight of stairs to apartment 2D than the old rickety elevator that was always breaking down; when caught between floors, you had to ring the alarm for Mr. Nash.

There were also the headlines, and now old enough to read the papers, the words "revoking of citizenship" and "deportation" filled me with apprehension, for many of us beginning a lifetime of recurring insomnia, that desperate escape from the unmediated demons of the night.

⊁⊀

For them, what remained?

In 1956, after the public admission by the 20th Congress of the Communist Party of the Soviet Union, when Khrushchev made his speech attesting to the tortures, frame-ups, unjust imprisonments, and executions of the Stalin era, Steve Nelson recalled, "I could see people, old Party leaders, crying in the audience. I said something like, 'This is not the reason why I joined the Party. From now on we have to reject this; we have to make our own decisions; there are no more gods.'"[1]

"Like ecclesiastics," George Charney wrote, "we had come to value dogma over experience."[2]

Toward the close of the story of his "journey," George manages to name both sides of what by the late 1950s and early 1960s had become the infamous contradiction. Marxism had appealed to him, to all of them, he wrote in passionate criticism and self-criticism, because it offered "a coherent explanation of all phenomena," a "theology," he called it. But he—they—also joined the Party and adhered to the philosophy that had given rise to the politics in so many places over so many years, "because of its ethical appeal and vision of freedom."[3] More than fifty years later, the foundation of this vision is still compelling to many, has played a central part in inspiring the struggle against tyranny across the Earth, including reforming American and European social policy. In 2016, during the primary contests for the presidential election, even the word "socialism" regained legitimacy, maybe even respect.

Bill had had doubts about Party ideology and Soviet domination since the 1920s, yet through it all he'd remained a loyal and even obedient member, a committed Party leader, swinging between years of commitment and then disagreement and accusation until he felt there was no choice left but to face the failure of the "instrument" if not the dream. Some old friends called it his Russian soul, others his Jewish temperament—an ingrained capacity to encompass contradictory emotions and philosophical oppositions without veering from a chosen path. I suppose since early childhood, perhaps since birth, he had lived with the character I knew for twenty-eight years—a tendency for fiery anger and an easy sinking into grief, but also a gift for analysis and balanced judgment. When I hear his laughter as I write this story, when I remember his silly jokes and self-mocking jibes, when I feel in my body his easy affection and full-hearted embrace, when I remember all this, I know he also possessed a sustaining, often joyous optimism.

There is a thin line, I have read someplace, between denial and hope, and if the former verges on dangerous naïveté, the latter is a virtue that gets one through. Despite years of depression and near breakdown, he carried this complex mix of temperament and intellect with him to his last days, attempting to preserve what remained.

><

A letter to his grandson Adam on the day of his first birthday:

SEPTEMBER 21, 1969.

In more than one way that was a beautiful day—for in the early hours of September 21, you made your appearance. In the months that followed you have given me unlimited joy and enriched my life. The night you were born I reached the height of ecstasy, a feeling I had the night your mother was born.

Throughout the years of her growth your grandpa encountered many difficulties presented by human life and a sick society. Her presence and that of her younger sister, your aunt, strengthened me in the battle for survival and served as an encouragement to conquer and defeat adversity. Your presence once again gives me that courage and lust for life. I fervently hope that yours will be a smoother path than that of your grandpa. Yet I know, life being what it is, you too will come across dirty roads as you plow your way into manhood. Your parents will strengthen you and prepare you to face, with the dignity of a man, the obstacles presented. But, as you mature, all will depend on you. Your own strength, spiritual, moral and yes ideological.

The contemporary state of affairs in our land and in the world, as you reach your first birthday, is not a very pretty picture. Unfortunately, despite the attempts by your grandpa and many others to present you with a better world, we were not very successful. Thus, it is left to your generation and that of your parents to blaze a new path, free of prejudice, hunger and wars. I know as you make your way through life you will be a pride to us all. Above all, to yourself.

There is a legend spread by your daddy and your uncle that the Lazarre tribe is verbose. And the champion of them all is your Grandpa Bill. So as not to give these guys a chance to perpetuate this legend I will limit this letter to a mere few thousand words. I trust that some day you and I may correspond and exchange our respective experiences in life. I may be 80 or 90 by then, but Bertrand Russell was 97. I do hope that yours will be a more joyful and decent world than the one I have known. I know that with dignity and strength you will withstand, and fight back, as you witness injustice.

> With a heart full of love,
> Your grandpa,
> Bill

About twelve years earlier, a response to a letter of mine, discovered during one of my periodic cleaning-out and reorganizing of my files. It was written when I was fourteen, traveling for an entire summer in Europe with a small group of friends, led by a teacher we had been fortunate to have in the fifth grade and with whom we retained an active friendship. Most of our time was spent in Italy, our teacher's second home. In some of the poorest streets of Naples, we were surrounded by child beggars. There was one child in particular who affected me—her dirty, scrawny hand stretched out for lire, her tiny voice pleading, "Prego, signorina, prego." She entered my dreams, where she still appears now and then—sometimes scratching on the refrigerator like a lost cat, hoping for food, sometimes banging on my door, pleading for entry. Sometimes she is just standing there, still and ragged, no story or scene placing her, her hair yellowed and mangy around her dirty face, her large desperate eyes staring at me until I wake with a start, at times in tears, rushing for my journal to banish my nightmares, much as my father did in different ways, leaning on some sort of faith in analysis, description—in words.

＊＊

"Your description of the Street of the Dutchess reminded me of La Strada," he wrote.

> What a shame—in a world of plenty and richness little girls should have to beg for a few cents. Yes, Jankie [his name for me], there is poverty in our country too. Just a few blocks from where we live. It need not be. Some day it won't be. What a beautiful world we shall have when little boys and little girls won't have to worry about their meals or lack of meals, when parents will have economic security and enough time not only to devote to their children but also to express and fulfill their aspirations in life. It is sad to witness human misery. But I am sure human progress moves forward. Here and there it is slowed down,

often at the expense of human beings. But history moves on, and no power in the world can stop it. Take it all in Sweetheart, observe, listen to people, learn, learn, learn. You will come home richer in outlook, more understanding of human experience and struggles. Greetings to the gang. I love you always.

And in the last line of a letter written to me when I turned twenty-eight, the last of my birthdays he lived to see, he writes these words: "My faith in mankind knows no boundaries."

PART VI *The Mutilated World*

Try to praise the mutilated world.
Remember June's long days,
and wild strawberries, drops of rose wine.
The nettles that methodically overgrow
the abandoned homesteads of exiles.
You must praise the mutilated world.

ADAM ZAGAJEWSKI, "TRY TO PRAISE THE MUTILATED WORLD"

CHAPTER 19

As if it were happening now—the long-ago elegant dining room table moved years before to the large kitchen, its polished wood worn down to a rough surface in places, covered with a plastic cloth she would have despised. When it was time for dessert their mother would call the children in—to tell about their day or to present new drawings to be framed in the special place on the wall she had reserved for "their work." Bourgeois pretentions, he sometimes felt (he smiled at the old word, in the sixties brought into use again by the "New" Left), but at other times he found it all endearing, and comforting too—the beautiful orderly rooms, colors carefully blended, a thick mattress on their wide bed. And whatever her preferences for material comforts, they were matched by extraordinary courage and commitment to the cause. She had risked her own safety more than once, carrying messages to European Party members at the behest of the American Party, responding to instructions from Moscow. Or she had taken those risks not primarily for an idea or principle but, he sometimes suspected, for him. It didn't matter anymore. All the better if she had done it out of love, considering how it turned out in the end.

As if it were all happening now, though he is sitting alone in his sturdy wingback chair, its fabric changed many times on his daughters' insistence about clashing colors, still in its old place in the living room—a calm room after all the transformations over the years. Tonight, all the versions seem visible to him, as if through a series of mirrors surrounding the actual room. The soft nubby gray cotton of Tullah's couch, used as a room divider to form the dining room she insisted on and loved to use, eating with him alone after a long day of work, beautiful dishes—even a small dish for bread and butter!—the girls kept in their room by their grandmother, or whoever was working for them at the time, eventually Rose.

As if she were sitting there now, in her favorite green velvet chair, its frame broken long ago, discarded as trash. As if the wallpaper she loved with its tiny green leaves still surrounded him—her attraction to all things British, its culture, its novels, the names she had chosen for her daughters—Emily, Jane. His sisters had laughed tolerantly, even admiringly—their elegant American-born sister-in-law—or perhaps with a silent feeling of loss? Their children named in the old way, no degree of secularism or even communist principles enough to erase certain requirements, habits kept, obligations fulfilled, names of the dead to carry on a legacy—Shirley, after Sliva, her grandmother, his mama, who had lived only a brief time in America; Miriam, for her paternal grandmother; Norman, in honor of Nissel, later called Nathan, the father whose daughters would not allow their brother to disparage, let alone condemn. Old-country Jewish namings, as close to the heart of Judaism as the endless laws and rituals, maybe as Torah itself; retained in spite of a secular faith as demanding as the ancient religion, he thought at times now, preserved across once unimagined geographical distances—the Kaddish prayer for his parents he never spoke, lately, astonishingly, causing him some guilt—generation after generation bearing and preserving names.

He leans his head back against the strong construction of wood and heavy cotton. He had marveled at the complexity of the interior with the upholsterer who came to recover the chair once again— "Don't make 'em like this anymore," he had said. Letting his thoughts roam he sees himself in the twenties, living in Philadelphia, at first with Mama and the father he still refuses to call "Father," even to himself—certainly not "Papa," no, Nissel, his name, more than enough respect in not calling him son of a bitch—then with his sister Leza and her husband David, later with Va. The first unhappy marriage of three— unless you count the early years with Tullah, before and just after the girls were born—until something had gone wrong, more than the horrible disease, and he had never known what.

He feels torn, as if it were all happening now. Jagged rips. Conflicts always battling within him. He had been decisive as a leader, he knew that—in the Party, in Spain—but inside, the rips.

Tullah's voice, some place between annoyance and loving concern—You are too aware of all the considerations all the time—give your brain a rest.

Your mind is very deep, it encompasses many levels at once—you can't shut your thoughts out—it's a blessing and a curse. Her. The woman he begins to think he will call Marian—the real name of Bender's wife, a sensitive woman, honest and loyal—that is, if he ever gets to the story he thinks he might try to write some day about his last departed love, for now she's gone too, her way of seeing him more tender, more complimentary.

All his life he had been an activist—it was a necessity, an inner certainty he had felt since early childhood—what he must do, what must be done. Yet always, beneath his organizing, his teaching, his leadership—the voices, questioning, debating, wondering, even doubting, suggesting different possibilities and alternative directions. Maybe he should have been a writer like his daughter was becoming. But he had not had that choice.

The worst tear of all began early, fifty years before, with Lovestone—Bukharin in exile in Paris, eventually murdered by Stalin. Socialism at a snail's pace, Bukharin had dared to say, arguing for peasants to be allowed to sell their own food and thus grow more prosperous before being forced into a permanent policy of collective farming. Eighty percent of the population of Russia was poor, devastated, now to be rushed, herded into farms where they would remain poor and devastated? Who knew for how long under those conditions they could maintain devotion to the Revolution? In the thirties, even before Spain, Bukharin had warned of fascism—its appeal in times of chaos.

Knowledge, old and current, swims in his mind like his mind is a moving river and memory a series of small crafts, floating, rocking on the waves, each one tied to the others.

Bukharin, a principal framer of the Soviet constitution with individual freedoms assured, then exiled, but for a good purpose at least—to retrieve the Marx and Engels archives held by German social democrats before Hitler could destroy them. Years later he wrote against forced collectivization at the wrong historical time—against complete obedience—grief and anger causing him to condemn—accused of disloyalty—exiled and imprisoned. Words that still sting, if memory serves, like he read them yesterday, and like all the loyal Party members he had scoffed at the words at the time—They are no longer human beings—They have become cogs in a terrible machine—frightening words. True? He doesn't know. In a way he no longer cares. He'd dismissed, even despised Bukharin—now the words seem to be—possibly could have been—from all he has witnessed and had to accept—might have been close to the truth.[1]

Words—thoughts—like shouts in his mind all these years later, after so many events and revelations that changed his life and the life of his comrades—some in despair, others enraged at their own history, their own failures to see, and blaming the failure on others—liars, hypocritical opportunists, power obsessed maniacs they called them now. But he cannot blame the tyrants and dictators alone, not entirely. There were overwhelming forces—poverty, the threat of invasion, a long history of tyranny—confronting the young revolution. He had believed. They had all wanted desperately to believe.

Overlapping stories of his life converge, separate, mix up again. He can't sleep and he can't read—all he seems able to do is stare, letting the confusion have its way. At some point, he thinks—shifting position, then standing to peer out the window at the night, eased a bit by the lights in the buildings across the street—others too unable to sleep tonight—at some point something might become clear. A Lovestonian someone had called him, derisively. Jay Lovestone, expelled long ago, a century ago it sometimes seems, then like yesterday, for his sympathy with Bukharin. Then Browder came in—and things seemed maybe not so bad—a sensible direction. Browder—to the end a believer in what he called American exceptionalism. He smiles ruefully—taps the windowpane. The idea seemed reasonable at the time, lately seemed so again—since American capitalism was not about to fail and revolution was not anywhere in sight— alliances with other progressive forces were both desirable and strategic. That much at least had been correct—the Great Depression had brought the idea into disrepute but Roosevelt's New Deal had repaired so much—though they had to fight for it, demonstrate, be arrested, and for what? For demanding social security and an eight-hour day—he has photos someplace in the house— all of them marching, shoved into police vans, cuffed. He had probably mocked such possibilities himself in '28 when he appealed his conviction in Philadelphia— he had mocked it, any thought that capitalism could heal itself, and spent time in prison for his words. He had even written a denunciation of Lovestone in an article he wrote with Browder—connecting the Lovestonians to other condemned parties of the left—Trotskyites, Norman Thomas socialists—some of the splits in Spain. Progressives called reactionaries. And maybe they were in a way—he still believes they played a part in the loss to Franco and the fascists, the Popular Front thrown out like so much garbage. He had revered Roosevelt—you always had to bring pressure from the Left, but he had been loyal to the idea of democracy in his heart, to the New Deal. They had all believed—that together . . .

And yet . . .

All the fights turning more and more impenetrable—filled with hate. Back and forth.

Forth and back, must be the correct way to say it, he had insisted to his daughters—you walk forth first, then back—he had kept it up, his insistence, letting them enjoy teasing him for his old-country speech.

Backing away from the window, he paced the room a few times, then sat down again. A book he remembers, out of nowhere—he had read it to them years ago, when they were children and Tullah had just died. He had to somehow learn the bedtime rituals she had begun and followed religiously when she was home—first stories, then songs. Something about Molly—it comes back to him now—Molly irons her clothes, nice and smooth. But his pronunciation always a bit off—his English carrying the old-country sounds—sounds in his own ears now and in his long ago voice—Molly irons her clothes, nice and smuth. His mispronunciation sent his daughters into such wild hilarity he had kept it up, pretending he didn't hear the difference—What? Smuth. I said smuth. Why are you laughing? Making them laugh even more.

Too much thinking, too fast, uninvited fragments of memory—he shakes himself awake from the dreamlike state he has fallen into, stands up again, this time goes into the kitchen to get a glass of water, long ago abandoned his small fast swallow of scotch to chase the bad thoughts away making possible some kind of relaxation. Remnants of arguments with comrades, fears of the FBI. Money worries, always that. The creeps, he had begun to call them, using his daughters' word. He has them now. Too many thoughts. Too many memories. The creeps.

He returns to his chair, picks up the newspaper he has not finished reading. But the printed words swim like the memories and again he stares, as he often does once his daughter and son-in-law are gone to their temporary home in Connecticut, stares at the newly painted bookshelves, relieved that the bright red Maurine had painted them with her usual excessive taste for the dramatic was covered up now with a clean white.

He is lonely—too honest and too accustomed to its burdens to deny it. One way and another he has been lonely since Tullah died—even with the women who followed, finally Maurine. None of them, much like Va in Philly all those years ago—none of them somehow touched his heart, though they were good women. Mary—nurturing, apparently very much in love with him, or so she said, raising three kids on her own after her own young husband suddenly died—but he could not feel anything but friendship for her no matter how hard he tried, even with his girls pushing him, "Marry Mary, Marry Mary"—her daughters their new best friends, her uptown apartment a second home, and Mary herself—even with chronic drinking—he didn't want to count the scotches she downed every night—treated them with such full and open love he could almost see the two families becoming one, the girls with a mama again, himself a father to her kids. But he could not get any sexual feeling for her—felt no desire for physical love. And before her—a lineup of young, dark-haired women, artists, teachers, women who stimulated his desire—but always there was something wrong—they were too dominating, or not political, too withdrawn or fighters about everything—like he could be at times—he wouldn't deny it—but he had taught himself with tough self-discipline to—most of the time—control himself. He did not want to double or triple such open conflict in his home. He longed for Tullah, dead for almost two decades now—her self-control came to her naturally—a kind of elegant calm that matched her clothes, even her bathrobe made of pink silk, her bedroom slippers—striped with blue velvet and silver—did they even keep her feet warm? All her clothes—like her rooms—carefully designed. Yet she was passionate, an ability to talk and converse in so many situations, but then—those awful silences when he wanted more than anything her words.

He'd never really known how to interpret the silences—they seemed to contain so many different meanings—an internal quiet he could only envy? Stubbornness? An unwillingness to argue he could not penetrate no matter how hard he tried, how loud he screamed himself at times. At times so irrational, as if she refused to think things through. She terrified the girls with her fear of mice—tiny unthreatening creatures—he could easily get rid of the occasional one that appeared in the kitchen—but nothing convinced her, she would not even discuss it—she grabbed the kids and pushed them into the bedroom, slamming the door until he shouted it was "safe" to come out. Safe? It was ridiculous— yet somehow also appealing. At times he felt he was being condemned, critical and disdainful words filled his one good ear as if she had spoken, as if he could read her mind, which he was humble enough to doubt. She'd change the subject to something lighter, something they agreed on. He felt ignored, angry. And at other times he found it appealing, comforting, dignified, even erotic.

Maurine seemed at first a kindred spirit and at the same time exotic. An actress, a Christian, raised in Texas, joining the Party out of the same convictions about human destiny he cherished himself. But her taste for dramatic colors paralleled her taste for dramatic argument. Well, she was an actress, a red-haired American shiksa—he had certainly deceived himself that time, and yet held on for years, living with shouts and explosions, another one always ready for a fight. First she had gone about changing the entire apartment—well, it was her right to do so—turning their bedroom into a study and rehearsal room so each night they had to pull out the uncomfortable couch-bed for sleeping, creating that sensationally ridiculous dressing room, its hooks and rods, its theatrical lights and large mirrors, now holding a couple of his ties, his few suits. He would never go in there to comb his hair or dress—he combed his hair before the old medicine cabinet mirror in his small shower room—his shower, his sink—and he dressed in his bedroom as he had always done, keeping most of his clothes in the closet he and Tullah had shared.

Then she had gone about trying to change him—arguments and accusations—about family traditions—lectures about child rearing—food—and politics, always that. Shouts filling the rooms, even when guests were present, instead of the peace he longed for. She was a victim of his past, she'd shout. She didn't want to be dragged into his depression with him—well he had to concede, she had a point there, he had a tendency to see the dark side, especially in recent years—she chose life, she'd shout, eyes blazing, fingers pointing, as if she were on stage, accusing him of a death wish. He sneers remembering, he who has never stopped trying to survive.

He had stuck it out, mostly because the girls were attached to her. They loved her fancy dressing room, the lights, the mirror, the costumes she let them wear. They seemed relaxed in a new way, at least in the beginning, as if they were freed of the burden—the burden of himself, he worries now, sliding deeper, he can feel it, into the depression that stalks him on this night like so many nights before. Because it must be partly—maybe mostly—his own fault—his failures with women—his failure to see.

He tries to focus on good memories. All good women, including Maurine. But none of them touched his heart, none of them moved his body. Not until—

Marian—he begins to think of her as Marian—coming to him in his advancing age—and now she too is gone.

The white bookshelves are neat, spaces filled with colored vases and old clay bowls the girls made in school long ago, no longer crowded now that Maurine's books are gone. He casts his eyes over the set of Lincoln's papers, a special edition given in appreciation to members of the Brigade. Six volumes of Carl Sandburg's poems, American literature and Soviet novels mixed in with Russian classics, contemporary political and social analysis, popular fiction to take his mind off everything and help him sleep. But nothing will work tonight. Tonight for some reason he is living in the past, the very thing he has always lectured his friends one should not do.

Bukharin. Lovestone. Browder.

Philadelphia. Ellis Island. Even Kishinev.

One or two times in those early years, the twenties—he guesses—he had almost lost faith. A terrible fight with Va. Why? Had he threatened to quit the Party? He seems to remember that. He can see her now—hear her old-country accent matching his own—pacing the floor, throwing things, magazines, a book nearly hit him in the head. "No you won't!" she had shouted—"You never will, and you know it!"—hollering at him words he knew were the truth. He has no clear recollection of the content of the battle, only that it was one of those that led to eventual divorce.

But Va was right. He hadn't quit then. He had kept on and breathed some relief when it was Browder taking over. Years later, when George and the others had lost faith entirely, speaking out for a liberal socialism they had once disdained, he had hung on again, thumping his chest as he spoke, he remembers now with a smile, in his best exhorting tones—communist blood coursing through my veins—while the others invoked their Jewishness. Even after the Holocaust, wondering who from his own youth and childhood were left alive, who burnt to ash in the horrific camps, whose bones mixed to unnamed dust in mass graves, whose skin made into lampshades, maybe still lighting the room of some old Nazi—even after all that—especially after that—his belief in internationalism had deepened—the only hope, the only cure for mankind's bloody history of hatred and war. But for many of his trusted comrades, being Communist Internationalists was not enough. Suddenly, Jews.

Persecutions, imprisonments, killings—anti-Semitism steeped in Russian history, running like blood through the veins of Russian life, gathering in great pools of poison in many Russian hearts. He had no trouble remembering the Cossacks. Easily he is slipping back to Kishinev—everyone talking about the pogroms, whispered fears and vague words that later became well-known history as he grew older, listened, and read—vicious rumors about Christian children killed by Jews in ritual murders, anti-Semitic incitements, riots, "rivers of Jewish blood"—the phrase used in so many newspaper reports. He was Jewish in every way except in the religious sense. Sitting in his sisters' kitchens in Philadelphia when the girls were small and Tullah just dead, the comfort and pleasure of eating the old-country food, his sisters competing for who could feed him best, baking and roasting the meals he never got at home. Speaking Yiddish to Sema's father-in-law in his long coat and hat never removed, his white beard flowing over the black clothing—laughter and arguments reminding them all of old times. He whispers a few of the old Yiddish phrases now, like he's talking politics again with his brother-in-law, Lyova. They lean over the long work table where Leon, as American friends call him, makes his beautiful quilts—a large one he'd slept under for years, no longer—must have worn out—and small ones for doll carriages he hopes his daughters still save, tucked away in some closet, waiting for little girls of their own. They talked into the night, arguing, reminiscing, trying to put it all together into some understandable story, this never achieved.

He'd had a choice like so many Jews. Zionism, with its new radical demands for Jewish retaliation, plans for mass returns to Palestine—many already there, settling and working the land like their ancestors, finally leaving Jew-hating Europe and Russia behind. Or Communism, his choice—internationalism his "religion"—perhaps an apt word—his people the workers of the world.

Yet his Jewishness never in question—all he has to do is look into the mirror and see his own face—obviously Semitic despite the fair coloring and blue eyes. Jewish. It's who he is. But not who he chose to be, since the age of thirteen in the old country when he learned and found hope—all nations and religions united only by their shared humanity, the people who created all the wealth of the earth finally owning it, owning it together.

He winces at the old rhetoric, recaptured easily like an old song. Like the old lady dying in a story his older daughter had recently insisted he read—Eva, the character was called—something about a riddle— "Still you believed?"—it was her husband who asked. He's like Eva. He too still believes.

He is walking in the hills of Kishinev again, the whole world changed by the brilliance of all he is reading, as if walls were literally breaking down to let light in, all that is happening around him, in the synagogues, in the streets, in the whispering he overhears in his old man's tearoom. Everywhere.

"The history of all hitherto existing societies is the history of the class struggles." That stunning declaration—opening the Manifesto.

These books and the ideas they brought into the world are the only paternity he has ever known, the only patriotism he has ever believed in. Rereading them many times so he wouldn't miss a thing. Those old books long gone now. Too heavy to lug to the train and then to the ship that brought them to America. But he had lost no time replacing them with English translations once he had mastered the new language that had taken him not so long. Not long at all. And when he reread them in English, the same excitement, the surge of faith, betrayed by many, even Stalin, in whom he had once so fully believed. But the ideals, those he had never betrayed. He can feel it even now, the old exultation of belief.

> *Arise ye prisoners of starvation—*

Some voice—his own?—suddenly audible. Many voices raised in unison, masses of people singing. He often sings when he is alone, so maybe without knowing it, in this lonely state of half-conscious meditation, he has begun to sing?

> *Arise ye wretched of the earth,*
>   *for justice thunders condemnation . . .*

He wants to sing, but even all alone, he feels embarrassed. The old vision, the lost hopes, hopes that obscured even reason—the human capacity for thinking clearly—like the scientists whose methods they revered, wanted to, tried to apply to social organization, to messy increasingly incomprehensible human relations—their illusions could still shake him with shame. Still, he hums, thinking the old words,

> *A better world's in birth . . . something, something—*
>   *let each stand in his place,*
>   *International Union—*

that was the line, he is singing it,

> *shall be the human race.*

The night has worn itself into early morning and he wonders what has resurrected such a mountain of feeling, anger at his disinheritance as strong now as the day in '58 when he officially resigned his post in the Party. Not much of a post by then, but he had given everything to it, sacrificed so much out of the most powerful love he had ever known—until Tullah, and the girls. One more time, sitting in the nice reupholstered chair, he lets himself sink back, time—past and present—swimming again.

Reds—the red flag—bandera rosa—avanti populo—the Italian comrades singing. Calling Maurine "Red" for her hair and her politics in the early days, when they were in love, when they all still believed. Those red bookshelves—he smiles, remembering—Reds, they called themselves proudly.

Koba, why do you need me to die?

Bukharin's last letter—using Stalin's revolutionary nickname—kept for who knows what reason by Stalin and so found in his desk in 1953 when he died. Leafing through a volume of Bukharin's letters recently he had come upon these devastating words.

And now, unable to sleep, reliving, reliving—for what reason?

Others asked him. He asks himself. For what other reason? Why else?

To understand.

CHAPTER 20

I am sitting in the same wingback chair that belonged to my father, rereading notes and drafts, research gathered in a series of black notebooks now kept for more than five years, trying to understand the way historical forces can take hold of our personal lives, swing us back and forth between action and acceptance of the limits of everything.

The chair is now a rich burgundy with a very slight touch of rose. It took me a long time to choose the color when I had it reupholstered once again last year. It has been white brocade—the first fabric I remember from my childhood—much later the green-checked heavy cotton my father brought home from the fabrics company where he worked. Even in my own living room it has changed often over the years, from thick white linen to a dark tan cotton, once its graceful lines and curves hidden by a badly fitted slipcover of an unsatisfactory rosy pink. Now the dark wine red—a color I love.

I reread and savor my father's letters, always encouraged in my own dark times by his sustaining fidelity to *fundamental values*. I have taken up his habit, now often carried on in email, of writing long letters to friends, sons, my granddaughter who once remarked, "I love your letters, Noni, but they are so long!" Forty-four years later, I am still amazed by his honesty, first blunt, then infused with familiar rhetoric, then stirring, as if emotion and idea were new and inspiring, unscathed by history. I struggle to attain his capacity, confronted by disappointing realities of many kinds, to retain hope.

∗∗

Summer 1968: Douglas and I are recently married and we are sitting in the New York airport with my father at a time when coast-to-coast flying is more rare for most people than it is now. We are waiting a bit nervously for our flight to San Francisco. Then we will cross the long bridge to the East Bay, where my sister and her soon-to-be-husband now live in Berkeley. I am not yet pregnant. In his midtwenties, Douglas will begin his law studies at the prestigious Yale Law School in a month—a wonderful shock for him and his family—no one in their world at that time having considered such a swift, long leap across two or three economic classes into potential privilege. Douglas has never before been to school with white students, not in the Catholic elementary school in his hometown where he had been enrolled by his mother after her conversion from The Disciples of Christ, in part so her children could attend a school that was equally segregated but academically superior to the colored public school in town; not in the high school for blacks; not in the historically black college in Durham, North Carolina, where he completed his BA and one year of law school, working his way through by waiting tables at the still completely segregated Duke University, a few miles away on Tobacco Road.

My father's early doubts about his new son-in-law had gone through a few stages and tests. In the early years of our relationship before we were married, my father sent an emissary to my apartment uptown to evaluate and report. Arthur Birnkrant, a blacklisted film writer and also a talented artist—he was always sketching—was also our godfather. The unusual distinction for an atheist Jewish family was applied along with many other rituals and customs to accommodate to the largely Christian nation in which we lived—one of the ideals of the Communists being to respect and hopefully recruit members from that world. There was the yearly Christmas tree, the Easter baskets and singing of "In your Easter bonnet, with all the frills upon it," which my grandmother and her sister quickly changed to "In your Pesach bonnet, with all the tchotchkes on it," and there were Arthur and his wife Ruthie, our godparents. There had of course been no Christening—they would not have gone that far—but Arthur, with no children of his own, took his godfatherhood seriously in many ways.

With the other young Communist children, we were allowed to call him whenever we had an argument with our parents about bedtime, or extra dessert, or other equally serious matters, and he would represent us (he was a trained lawyer among other accomplishments) for a nickel, winning many cases for us over the phone. In my uptown apartment, which I had begun to share on many nights with Douglas, the bell rang unexpectedly, and there was Arthur at the door—just one of the typical unannounced visits he made to all his friends, "just to have a talk"; he "happened to be in the neighborhood." It was of course clear to me immediately that he had been sent by my father to observe and report on my new love. And he did, giving Douglas a more-than-passing grade that he somehow ascertained in an hour of a discussion the details of which I have no memory at all. He was the member of the Cultural Region who first taught me how to draw faces and gave me the proper pencils with which to obtain not only lines but shadings so that faces had planes and shadows, rings under tired eyes, wrinkles suggesting age. Later, after my father's death, he and another long-time friend from Party days would help me publish my first book, providing what most writers need—some sort of connection, which they had. Many years later, not long before his wife, our godmother, died, she gave me a personal copy of his manuscript, *A Plea, a Confession, a List, and Assorted Vagaries,* pages of suggested bibliography and commentary, all neatly typed and personally bound, lists and interpretations I still consult today.

By the time we decided to marry, any early doubts my father entertained about Douglas, which were actually doubts about myself—my lifelong tendency, in his view, to "jump into things without thinking them through"—had passed, erased by their burgeoning friendship founded on shared values and interests, enhanced by pride in his admission to the law school at Yale, a citadel of America's Ivy League. The promise embedded in this event was almost as remote to my immigrant, formally uneducated father as to my in-laws, all of them now confident of a secure and comfortable life ahead for us both.

No one can finally explain the nature of any attachment. However long or thoughtful a list we make there is always something else, unnamed and not fully known. This was true, I believe, for my father and my husband. They shared something elusive—something to do with an attraction between Russian Jewish emotionalism and the careful discipline and control internalized by many African American men.

Douglas's family had accepted me more readily than I expected, and there was no objection at all in my father's mind to "interracial" marriage, though there were other members of my family who raised many of the usual questions, from "concern about the children" to more outright racist objections. If my father had to argue with or defend me to any of them, I never knew of it. And although I still had a great deal to learn about race and racism in America, a transformation in consciousness I would write about in several future books, at the time it was Douglas's steadfast reliability, emotional stability and profound capacity for love—somehow provided for him by a large and intimate extended family with his mother and father at the center—that drew me to him and draws me still. Now, after close to fifty years have faded any meaning to our skin color difference except in public situations, I suppose there was some exoticism in each of us for the other, a difference in culture and history that augmented our love.

Remembering my father's exuberance at having a male grandchild, I think there was also a certain masculine camaraderie he relished and missed in never having a son. A mother of two sons I could not love or admire more than I do, I experienced a unique feeling of joy—in continuity? in the hope of that special intimacy girls and women sometimes share?—when my granddaughter was born.

><

At the airport in the 1960s, still bare of the now proliferating elite shopping opportunities, coffee is available, a doughnut, and, as always, my father's early morning bible—"The Papers"—and he opens his ubiquitous *New York Times*.

The Soviet Union has invaded Czechoslovakia, deposing the progressive Dubček, who had promoted democratization and civil liberties as part of a plan to decentralize government, making it more responsive to peoples' needs. Like many comrades and former Party members, Bill had followed the Prague Spring with rekindled hope and admiration for Dubček. Now he is reading about invading Russian tanks, about occupation. He is devastated. All the betrayals come back to him. Soviet imperialism, the squashing of other Eastern European democracies, — Tito, scorned and vilified for criticisms of Stalin's Soviet Union—and now, Czechoslovakia too, Soviet tanks in Prague. He can't take his eyes off the newsprint, reads the articles again, reads paragraphs out loud to us. He shakes his head. Tears run over his lids and cloud his glasses so he has to remove them, take out the still ubiquitous wrinkled handkerchief to wipe both lenses and eyes. "Ruined" is the word that comes to my mind. Years later, I will discover the poem by Adam Zagajewski and know that in that moment my father was being tested as strongly as he'd ever been to love and praise his mutilated world.

Then he had no words. We sat in silence during long minutes until we were called to board our flight.

I don't remember what may have happened next, what we may have discussed during the six-hour flight, or if we remained silent in our own seats, smoking (legal everywhere then, the widespread disastrous health reports still in the future), all of us nervous but also excited to be in the air on our way to a West Coast state none of us has ever seen before. The New Left is in full swing, its denunciations of American militarism and racial injustice nearly matched by its denunciations of Bill's generation of radicals, its own splits, which will get much worse in the months and years to come, perhaps even more wrenching and destructive than theirs have been.

I do remember the more pleasant, easier parts of that journey west—the happiness we both felt in being reunited, even for a short visit, with my sister, the daughter he never ceased missing, the girl I loved more than I then even knew. During that visit to my sister's small comfortable house in the Berkeley flats, my father was enchanted by the university town itself, by her lawn and chaise lounge where, whenever the fog lifted, he baked in the sun for hours, heedless of the burning of his fair skin, his shirt hung over the back of his chair, his chest and face drenched in sweaty pleasure. But all that week he must have been thinking of Czechoslovakia, Hungary, Yugoslavia. He must have been suffering agonies of revisionist doubt, anger, and shame.

I think very often of those intense, chaotic times, the movements for justice and for peace of my father's generation and my own, rivalries as deep and sometimes as vicious as the worst sibling baggage, weighing down relationships for years, threatening friendship, ending many. I have no illusions that I can discover or frame a coherent history. After experiencing dramatic transformations in awareness and consciousness about the realities and meanings of historical events during the Civil Rights and Feminist movements—how these changes have affected the way we *know,* how we read, how we understand ourselves and the world—I don't even believe there is such a thing as some final "coherent history," not if that seductive phrase suggests a vision of the past as orderly as a clear map leading from one place to another, highways, bridges, alternate routes marked in red and black ink.

Having grown up and into consciousness within the protective, loving, but ultimately devastated world of the American Communist Party, I turned to writing stories—some taken from real life though altered and rearranged, some recreating emotional if not literal experience—always in an effort—sometimes conscious, at other times subliminal I assume—to get at something true.

Some stories emerge from characters I know or knew; some are composites of two or three people in whom I sense some intriguing connection; some are direct or indirect self-portraits; some are from who knows where. All stories change and alter as they expand and grow, but I do not experience the process as magical, nor can I assert ignorance of all sources. I was told once by a student of mine that the writer Grace Paley, with whom she had previously studied, insisted on the word "story" rather than the too-often-misunderstood word "fiction." All stories have their sources in both experience and imagination, in explicit and faithful recording as well as in what we call "making things up." Sometimes they are simply what Doris Lessing once described as "writing down what happens." When they are written in a certain evocative way, when the writer searches for language used as precisely and lyrically as music, when structures are created to reveal meaning and suggest unspoken layers of reality, they are called fiction. But memoir too can achieve harmonic blending of meaning and form, inevitably includes reliable as well as uncertain memories evoked by a single word or shaped by a sustaining image—that word itself the root of the word "imagination."

I imagine the grandmother of my father, the woman he slept beside for I don't know how many years. I feel his body warmed by hers and by the hand-sewn quilt left behind in Kishinev when she herself was left behind, never to be seen by her family again, never again to see her daughter, her grandchildren, her little Itzrael, the sensitive one, the one who may have screamed from dreams in the night. I imagine my father's childhood when

I see the dramatic similarities between him and my younger son, a grandson he never knew, a boy who was also subject to bad dreams, who shouted nighttime fears he later calmed and controlled with a dedication to activism, service to others, and study. I imagine the youth on the SS *Kroonland*, taking care of his parents and sister, the brave young man facing judges and jury in a Philadelphia trial when I witness my older son's resilience and spirit in the face of life's difficulties. In both sons' love of family and intellectual dedications, I presume to imagine my father's inner life.

I have one photograph of my great-grandmother in a family portrait taken before anyone left for America. She wears the traditional babushka, hiding all her hair. Her face is chiseled, strong-looking, almost masculine. Other children stand around and in front of their parents. I can recognize one of the eldest daughters, my Aunt Leza whom I knew in Philadelphia. The older boy with eyes so intense they are striking even in the old brown-tinted photograph must be Uncle Buck who stands near his mother, a rope-belt tied around his waist, a book in his hand. A younger girl looks a bit like Rose, and a smaller child with long bangs hanging below her eyebrows must be Sema, the youngest—she sits in her grandmother's lap wrapped in a large blanket or cloak. And there is my father, standing stiffly in front of his father, who looks severe and grim (it might be the discomfort of being photographed, for they all look grim, or it might be the character my father repeatedly described). His hand rests awkwardly on the shoulder of his son.

I stare at my grandmother, uprooted from home and mother, and—who knows—maybe wanting to leave so she could see her daughters again for all the risks and abandonments that entailed, to be with Leza and Raisela, to escape the anti-Semitism so prevalent and threatening in the country of her birth. She would die in the strange city of Philadelphia not long after she arrived, barely settled, much too soon to see even her oldest grandchildren, and no one, not my surviving older cousins nor any records I have been able to find, can tell me where she and my grandfather are buried.

As always in our life, politics and family loss run together, like a wash of watercolor paint blending from outline to center with no clear boundary in between. I construct and reconstruct time lines, hoping that in the spaces between events—carefully and accurately listed, revised and corrected by subsequent readings, unburdened by premature interpretation—memory will be enticed once again, and some convincing, if not always literally accurate, story may emerge.

⇥⇤

During the summer of 1969, when I was seven, eight, then nine months pregnant, the heat wave slowing me down and even causing one fainting spell, I was not concerned. In those days we were not forbidden alcohol when pregnant, so often in the evening I enjoyed a cold glass of sangria, learned to love chilled white wine. I can still feel the relief of the one small air-conditioner in my father's small bedroom where we gathered in the evenings to talk or watch the news on his small television. I wonder now why he never moved into the larger room that once belonged to my sister and myself, even though we were both gone from home. Perhaps he felt comforted by the familiar space he had slept in for decades or, since sleep for him was often elusive, where he either read or watched the news. Perhaps he was exhausted by the thought of moving all his books into another room and wanted them at hand, surrounding him. The shelves of leather-bound texts by Marx, Engels, and Lenin were no longer kept behind thick curtains, where they had been hidden during the 1950s from possible searches by the FBI, a futile enterprise if anyone came looking for hidden books, yet seemingly prudent during those paranoid and genuinely dangerous times. A collection of the great Russian and American novels he had read and re-read since the days in the Pennsylvania penitentiary years before; fiction by Soviet writers, Gorky, Boris Polevoi's *A Story about a Real Man*, a romantic story of a Soviet war hero, the worn blue leather-covered book still on my shelf; American and European Leftists—Malraux, Howard Fast—books he assigned to me for "reading and discussion" through my childhood and teenage years—all of these he continued to treasure, most of them read before his children were born, before Tullah, even before Spain. He would lie on the single bed he had bought to replace Maurine's sleeping couch when she moved out, one large lamp turned on behind him, always reading, and if we—my sister and I, later my husband and I—came in to talk, he would turn toward us, remind us to speak loudly, in the direction of his good ear, the other useless from the never-explained early injury that had destroyed his eardrum and kept him out of the army during World War Two, but not out of Spain, where there were no such standards.

At that time in my life, I was a graduate student in anthropology, hoping to use this degree as entrée into one of the less traditional psychoanalytic institutes. I did not worry then that my desire to write would conflict with these professional preparations. My son was not yet born, and ignorant of the demands of motherhood—in 1969 still veiled in mysteries of maternal instinct and mythologies of easy physical and psychological labors—I assumed I could do everything. I had completed one unpublished novel. I wrote essays for my courses that broke rules of social science discourse and veered into story. Still, writing outside of academic nonfiction seemed ancillary, something I connected to my love of reading but not something on which I hoped to build a working life. This was before the professionalization of the art of writing in MFA programs, before the inclusion in most undergraduate curricula of "creative writing" courses and thus the need for writers to teach them. In my world, it was assumed you would write if you were driven to do so, indeed, you would be honored for your passion and your talent, but you had to earn a living too. Most of us took courses in the education departments of the colleges we attended. I had used a "temporary substitute license"—then often providing a position that could last one or more years—to teach high school English before I moved to New Haven with Douglas and decided to apply to graduate school.

Those evenings, as the small air conditioner drew a cooling breeze into the room, I was not thinking much about my career choices. I kept up my classes in a vague hope to earn a PhD eventually, earn my living as a therapist, write too, I was sure. I was not conscious of much apart from the voices of father and husband as the baby's body inside me surged and rolled, kicked and quieted down again. Yet I must have been adding barely realized thoughts and images to my father's words, picturing the situations he was describing in scenes, for they return to me now as I make notes from notes, writing and revising, as I sit in his chair remembering two interlocking stories from that time.

≫≪

Greenwich Avenue forks into 6th, and Bill takes the right fork to the newsstand run by Johnny, an old comrade from the old good fights. See what the Western press is making of the Smith Act trials, a few of the accused still his friends. He clicks his tongue anticipating the distortions. A grey-suited man walks toward him; the loping confident stride, attractive face—Christian, American; the smile, inviting, as if in friendly recognition, only the slight tilt upward of the corners of his mouth suggesting something more sinister.

"Mr. Lazarre—excuse me—Lawrence—which do you prefer these days?" The man gives a soft salute, as if he is tipping his absent hat, as he offers the choice of names.

"How do you do, sir." He returns the greeting politely as always, as always evades the questions that inevitably follow the greeting, trying to catch him off guard. A pathetic ruse. He marvels at their stupidity, how long it takes them to figure out the simplest things. For five years believing he had an alias, sometimes Bill, sometimes Buck Lazar, and two apartments, one in Brooklyn, one here in the Village. Five years until they stopped greeting him with that one: "Good morning, Mr. Lazar—off to Brooklyn for the night?"

Didn't figure it out until they saw him with his brother—two handsome Jews, both prematurely white-haired, both with striking blue eyes and skin that turns pink in the sun. Both Communist leaders, Itzrael now Bill and Itzaac nicknamed Buck. Now Buck was dead, a heart attack at forty-nine, like their brother Dovedal—David, appendicitis before the discovery of penicillin, like their parents buried in America after only a few years' of reunion with their elder daughters, of freedom from poverty and pogroms, like his wife, wasted away from breast cancer no one could treat, let alone cure.

><

"She wouldn't let me see her in the last weeks, wouldn't allow me into the room, to hold her, what was left of her, to whisper my undying love and unbearable sorrow—only her sister and brother-in-law would she let into that dark room."

My father told me of this banishment during a visit the following summer, when my son was about eight months old. Twilight slowly darkening the living room, he reached behind him to turn on an old copper-based lamp, perhaps seeking to assuage the dark thoughts so often accosting him, but he looked away from my eyes, across the room toward the built-in bookshelves, then down into his lap, an unfocused gaze. I sat on a new black leather chair and matching ottoman he had purchased for me the previous fall so that during our frequent visits I could comfortably nurse my baby, an activity that had recently come back into repute for new mothers, but one that embarrassed my father.

"No one was doing that when you were born," he insisted—his "no one" meaning the early feminists or Communist women in the world he had known, certainly not my mother, a "career woman" who stopped working only for several weeks after the birth of each of her daughters. But the nursing seemed to please him, too—perhaps returning memories of his own mother nursing his younger sister in the old country.

"I was banished," he said, looking past me, nearly twenty years after the fact his eyes filling with tears.

My insistent question—"Why?"—went unanswered. He shook his head.

"I never knew," was all he said.

Crucial stories, entire chapters lost, always disturbing to me, ground-splitting.

But among the joys of our son's first years for his grandfather was Adam's ability to talk. One of those striking early speakers, he could manage full sentences before the age of two, and his grandfather, that language lover, writer, speech maker, and teacher, never tired of bragging to his friends about his grandson's precocity with words. "You can actually have a conversation with him," he'd report to Bender.

I salvage and preserve the image of his getting down on his knees each time we arrived from New Haven, Adam running down the hall to the doorway shouting, "Grandpa!" and throwing himself into my father's opened arms. He dreamed of Adam often, he told me, and often the dreams included scenes about race that may not have penetrated his dreamworld before. He would be signing into a hotel, and they would refuse him admittance with his black grandson, so he would fight them, or walk out, waking in fury. Despite the Party's attentions to racial oppression, he was inevitably comprehending American racism more intimately than before. Perhaps there was a loosening of many feelings and secrets as he looked into the eyes of a new generation, a temporary relief of his always lurking depression. Four years later, I would witness my mother-in-law's similar passion for our younger son, Khary, whose birth followed only weeks after her husband's death. "He saved my life," she tells us to this day. And remembering her now, slowly moving back and forth in a newly bought rocking chair with Khary draped over her shoulder, humming and whispering to him as she strolled around our apartment with what always seemed to me infinite patience, I see my father again, adoring Adam, his new life a temporary tonic for losses whose deepest scars would never fully heal.

Though for me the birth of my son began the healing of my lifelong conflicts with my father, conflict persisted, albeit in a lower register than before.

"Let Douglas hold the baby," he'd instruct me during Adam's infant crying bouts while I tried to comfort him—my father worried by his own anxieties, I suppose, as well as mine. But I was fortified by the start of what was clearly a good marriage, ardently obsessed, notwithstanding shock and various fears, with the radical love of new motherhood. I felt strengthened by my graduate classes and the research in which I was involved, resettled by a recently completed long psychoanalysis, and inspired by the fast-growing feminist movement. Through group meetings and written works we were digging out old oppressive ideas and painful memories, liberating feelings and voices, changing ourselves in that mysterious way powerful truths can achieve when they are new, or suddenly dug up, yet feel so long known and present they quickly become cliché: *Take back the night. The personal is political. Black is beautiful.*

Not least, I was only too happy to obey my father and turn the baby over to Douglas, with his calm nature and humorous acceptance of the ups and downs of life with an infant, a virtue not unlike his mother's, so I was neither as angry nor as hurt as I might have been in previous times. During the weekends and summer months spent with my father during those first years of Adam's life, my mind alternated with pictures of *Bill Lawrence,* heroic and brave, *Bill Lazarre*, defeated and sad, *Itzrael Lazarowitz,* young and committed to an international movement that for years seemed to many to be the revolutionary social system that would finally institute justice, eliminate poverty, and restore dignity to the working people of the earth. I could not have put it this way at the time, but I know now that during those summers I gave my love more freely than I had in many years. I felt forgiven by my father for my failures to measure up to old standards of my mother's elegance, his still severe criticisms of my lack of self-control. In his forgiveness of me, I began to forgive him too.

↔

"Pretty rough time, eh?" The handsome face of the FBI *operative smiles with a flash of what might be a moment of real sympathy. They are walking side by side now. Bill has turned right on Christopher Street, heading for a different newsstand, avoiding Johnny's.*

"Rough time? You mean the deaths?" He plays innocent, knows what they're after. A rough time—grief, betrayal—for their kind this leads inevitably to treachery. A stool pigeon they think he'll become.

"At the trial—the Party conventions—they betrayed you. Thompson insulted you, from what I hear."

He stares at the smooth face, marvels at the presumption. He holds back the absurd tears of rage that have always come too easily since he was a boy—his father's voice—"Haltn geshrign, Yisrael! Stop sniveling. You a man or your mama's little feygele?"—and a slap across the back of his head, which only made the tears flow more copiously. And now, that overgrown adolescent, Thompson, accusing him of treachery, even cowardice. He held back public tears, threatening, with the most willpower he could command.

He touches his forehead with his fingertips, mirroring the agent's salute. "I wish you good day, sir." He walks away, buys his paper, catches the bus on 7th heading downtown, jumps off at Bleecker at the last minute, just as the doors close, enters an apartment building, where he studies the bells until he sees the bus depart. No one follows him. After ten minutes or so he exits the building, grabs a coffee at the corner deli, two buttered rolls for the girls, one for his mother-in-law, and rushes back home to walk the kids to school.

><

In the wine-red chair in the corner of my own living room, rough drafts and old letters piled on a nearby table, I sat with my notebook writing in a longhand that in the days ahead would be transferred to a printed page. "Memoir about My Father" it was simply called for years, and it still bears that title in the earliest computer file. Why did she banish him, I wonder now, remembering. Any question about genre, truth, and fact, the distortions of memory by mistake or buried desire, are far from my mind. I will never know this story unless I imagine it from intuition fed by sounds and images that have inhabited my memories for years. My mind is filled with pictures and fragments of scenes. My nights are filled with dreams. He is young and powerful, calling to me as I run to him, invading my rooms as I shout at him. Or he is old and frail and I have neglected him, have forgotten to take care of him, and now I rush to his side. He is just a portrait in blue, or in shades of black and grey, a portrait his younger daughter might create, who did create many such drawings years ago. At times I wish I could abandon this work or finish it in a sudden burst of energy, letting both of us rest in peace again. But sentences come to me in the dark when I am longing for sleep. My mind is crowded with words.

Lower me into the dream house.
Dawn can pull me out.
Down there the dead can whisper.
Down there the dead can shout.

EUGENE MAHON, "NIGHT PRAYER" IN *ALL SERIOUS DARING*

He is frequently alone when he returns from the fabrics company where he now works. Dinners are last-minute affairs; tonight he picked up a pastrami on rye from the deli and his favorite dessert, a napoleon with custard filling. The evenings can be long. His daughter, son-in-law, and grandson won't return until the weekend, and it's only Wednesday. He takes out the yellow legal pad where he has dared to begin.

He will call her Marian, as planned. If he is going to attempt the act he's long imagined he'll follow the most traditional of fictional requirements: changing the names to protect the innocent.

So. Marian.

⊱⊰

She came into his life suddenly, a neighbor of Eddie Bender's, his best and oldest friend. (Later, he will change that name too, but for now, the only way he can picture it all is to call Bender by his real name—always just Bender, since Spain.)

She walked into Bender's small attached house in Queens, the recently widowed woman next door. His type—he could see that right away—on the petite side, dark hair—only a few silver streaks so it looked—and was he would discover natural. Olive skin with a hint of rose—not natural, but the makeup well applied. Casual clothing, nothing suggesting an involvement with appearance—

though he would learn she did care very much what she looked like, how she appeared to others. He liked this too.

How it was that after three important failures with women he thought he loved since the death of his wife nearly twenty years earlier that he was now able to enjoy physical love again, to perform acceptably (wonderfully, she said), to feel the old confidence he hadn't felt in decades—that enabled him to be—is "imaginative" the word, he wonders, crosses it out—to lose his self-consciousness, how this happened, he could never hope to comprehend. But it did. Over the course of the next year shameful memories began to fade—the passionate and angry painter he'd thought might be the one, the fiery actress he married and suffered with for five interminable years until mutual misery drove them apart, guilty memories of the nurse his daughter insisted would have made the perfect wife for him. "Face it Dad," she'd said, in that voice so full of certainty she reminded him of himself (she would have made a good party leader, he thought wryly, if he were young again, and she were not his daughter, if everything that had happened had not happened, he would have tried to recruit her). "You want to be taken care of! She's a nurse, she loves taking care of people!"—in her lecturing voice, not waiting for an answer. He did love Mary, but he felt as if he couldn't breathe when she embraced him, even when she talked about how close she wanted to be to him; no matter how close they became, she wanted to be closer, closer, until he felt he'd be devoured. All of it faded with Marian.

And she forced him—without meaning to, it seemed—to be different than he'd been before, or to be what he'd always wanted to be but couldn't be before, not even with Tullah.

(He'll change that name too, maybe—or maybe by calling her Tullah, her actual and unusual name, it will help him—help him finally to let her and his memories of her rest in peace?)

With Marian, he became more fully known to himself than he had ever been, as if lost parts of his life were coming back to him.

He dreamed of his grandmother, left to die alone in the old country. He saw her old face, her expressive eyes. He smelled the body he'd slept near his first five years of life.

He'd never written to her, she couldn't read anyway—still, he hoped his mother had written to a cousin to read aloud to her, or maybe his sisters had tried. He had never asked.

He had no interest in finding connections, "associations," his daughter called them, between the strange old memories in his recently vivid dreams and the joy he felt making love with Marian, the peace he found in her company through long quiet evenings, the excitement of a simple morning walk. She was too young for him, he told her, laughing ironically about the ten-year difference between them, because he knew he would fight to keep her against all odds. She scoffed. Age meant nothing, she said. She'd had a long marriage, filled with alterations between dull contentment and angry conflict. She couldn't have children, had only her sister, her niece and her nephew, and they lived on the west coast. She was in love for the first time in her life, she said, and—it was obvious—because he worked for an ordinary fabrics company, a small factory where he was called general manager but was really just one of the workers, cutting, folding, and labeling cloth—his days of revolutionary heroism were long behind him—she loved him not for his well-known radical charisma but for something else. Something old. Vulnerable—yet strong too, a strength he'd almost forgotten. Until it was there again, reminding him of Kishinev, the view of the city from the hills where he used to go to think and read, far away from his father and his tearoom, from what even then he knew was his mother's loneliness. He had dreamed of rescuing her somehow, though how or to where he had no idea. He remembered how he looked out at the city with its divided-up sections for gentiles, Jews, Turks, staring at the divisions and the ghettos, elaborate homes to one side, pitiful hovels to the other, and he would imagine the new world, a just world, free of poverty and despair.

And now it was over. Marian was gone, gone away to die far from him so he would not have to go through it again, she said, watching the woman he loved slowly waste away to skin and bone.

"Dead," her sister had written in the letter he received at the time. Then, his heart attack, months of recovery helped by his new grandson—reminding him that life did actually move on, his own life in some way continued. But here he was, still trying to get a hold on it after almost two years, or to hold on to her by writing, he couldn't tell which, only that it seemed to be true, like so many times in his life, all he had left were words.

Not a story yet, he realizes. Only notes.

So.

"The Story of Marian"

Another try.

Finally, a soul mate. Not a woman to adore or try to please, or to be frustrated by her lack of interest in ideas, in history—but spirit to spirit in the way he had only read about in books until now, an understanding that was immediate, even without the need for words.

Blessed, almost sacred. Could he use those words? He heard them in his mother's voice, its tones identical in later years to Rose's—even with all that anger she kept within and let loose on them all. But his mama's voice had been different—he could hear the sorrow, bitterness at times, but never harsh, never cruel, never cold. His sister never recovered completely, he supposes, from whatever happened to her long before, even after a life in America, marriage, a daughter, grandchildren. "She's mean," he had heard one of the girls say. But what makes someone mean like that?

"Nothing happens without the thing that happened before." His daughter had quoted the words proudly to him upon returning one day from a favorite high school history class. "That's what she keeps saying, Dad. Miss Teltcher. She points her finger at us and sort of smiles, and she says it, slowly, in a low voice, so we know she means us to write it down: Nothing happens without the thing that happened before."

He'd been proud of her love of what she was learning, that she wanted to find the less obvious meaning in things—to an extreme at times, but still, the search was there. Something lifesaving about the search itself—even when it led to high brick walls. When she was in college she'd become close to a group of psychology majors who though they all later switched to English novels remained Freudians, from what he could surmise, and she began to apply that intelligent perception about history to family history too. She'd shouted the words at him, "Our history too, Dad!! Nothing happens without the thing that happened before!"

"Que sera, sera," he had sung to her—the line from his latest favorite song, countering her excessive faith in rational analysis, in orderly movement from this to that. His life had taught him to distrust it as an absolute, to distrust any absolutes. Life itself, if lived long enough, threatens beliefs in order, predictability, fairness, beliefs that have driven him since he was a boy.

His mind is rushing from thing to thing, person to person, time to time, without any order or obvious meaning. He needs to slow down, get back to Marian. But his daughter interfered.

She was at that age when ideas were like being in love. The age he had been when he believed—well into his forties—wished he still believed—in the orderliness of it all, that if you dug deep enough, read widely enough, mastered both the sequences and the forces of history, of economic systems, if you really understood Lenin and Marx and did not get swept away by the need for power, by the cult of your own or someone else's personality, by the desire to control everyone—then, then, you might understand—in the next book, the next chapter, the next line of thought—all would be clear. Maybe it was not merely a wish but a remnant—like a piece of cloth too small to use, too beautiful to discard. Maybe something remained.

His daughter's ideas, her views about family and what she called "intimate life" had gotten to him, perhaps not altered his ideas completely but affected his perspective.

※

His mind is racing now, out of control like a wild horse, galloping from place to place—for he had begun writing about Marian and he wants to get back to her—instead these disjointed thoughts, yet maybe somehow connected? Cancer—part of the story—he can't avoid it.

The body he loved and adored, mutilated, then disintegrating before his eyes, month after terrible month, until the legs couldn't hold it up, the skin color changed—bones protruding as if about to break through the taut, fragile-looking skin—like old paper darkened to a deep yellow by age—the olive-gold skin he'd loved, that was like his mother's side, had missed all the children who favored their father's fair, blue-eyed, Slavic-looking family—all except Rose and David—Raisela and Dovadel—one dying young, the other living a life of buried feelings he'd never fully understand.

And it was not only the body, its sudden calamities, the early deaths that made no sense no matter how you tried to understand, but history itself. All the forces and outcomes that had turned everything around, turned comrades into enemies, friends into stool pigeons. George, one of his best friends, almost lost, and Harry, who had been seduced by the FBI. A stool pigeon. Stalin himself.

How to explain it? Character. History. The places where they met were no longer comprehensible to him. He either feared to know or was incapable of knowing. But Marian had understood.

And now he has found his way back to her.

※

Suddenly, she had been there, across the room from him, sitting upright in a straight-backed chair, her bathrobe tied tight around her, though it was a thin material and he could make out the outline of her breasts—she had understood.

She had moved so easily with him, like a dancer—he loved to dance, a waltz or a foxtrot around the living room—she understood his questions, shared his doubts about the old certainties, told him about all her wonderings, full of emotion, as passionate as their sex. She would begin to talk, picking up where his questions had left off. "I wonder," she said once, looking from him to the ceiling, the hallway behind him, back into his eyes. "I think about power, and powerlessness, and how there are things, Bill, we can never understand. We thought we could understand everything. We thought if we just read enough, found the right books and understood them well enough, we would know enough to actually change the world. If we analyzed carefully, and bravely, and were ready to make the right sacrifices, even sacrificing our own beliefs at times for the sake of the Party, then we could even see into the future, not only into the present moment but into the future, not merely imagine it, or want it, but really see. And once we saw it we could make it all happen, because we knew. And now, I am trying to understand what it means not to be able to know, that there might be forces—well—beyond our comprehension, or beyond comprehension itself, forces which have nothing at all to do with us—the most frightening thing of all..."

He had listened, and with no small degree of shock he had been deeply physically aroused.

History. The details and the large forces, its turns and reversals toward and away from justice defied his understanding, or suggested worse, far worse, just as she had said, that in some matters there was no understanding to be had. You had to proceed as if there were, he supposed, as if just around the bend, over the next hill, all would be clear and fall into place again, piercing through something dark and large to something small maybe, but clear enough to keep going on. Then he'd experience the old feeling one more time—in the tightly packed rooms in Kishinev where he'd first heard of Lenin's revolutionary words, the faith that had kept him going in Spain, in the grimy cell in the penitentiary in Philadelphia. For all the years, even behind the table at the HUAC hearing, with all the cameras flashing so he'd had to request—politely of course—for the committee members to ask them to stop so he would not have to turn his head un-

*comfortably away from them, so he could face his accusers, and as important—
so his face wouldn't be plastered all over the front pages of the* Post *or the*
News *or the* Mirror, *maybe even the* Times, *for his girls and their friends to
see—through it all, with small falls and backward steps, he had managed to
keep his faith, he had believed.*

*Now, it was different—not gone, but different. More conditional: Only if
and perhaps had taken the place of "inevitably." Justice was not only sacred,
it was fragile too. Science was not only beautiful, it could also be the ugliest,
cruelest force in the universe. Names raced through his mind, names bursting
at the seams with too much meaning. Hungary. Czechoslovakia. Hiroshima.
Stalin. Uncle Joe. Man of Steel. Mississippi. Vietnam.*

*Marian knew. When they talked he felt comforted to be accompanied, to be
known. Her body seemed like a part of his own. And then she was gone.*

*He would never understand. There was nothing to understand. Only to
absorb.*

><

*He puts down his pen, puts the yellow legal pad down on the desk. It has turned
into a meditation—a memory mixed up with too many unconnected feelings.
Not a story at all.*

><

In bits and disjointed pieces his words come back to me, the experience he
began to tell us about in fragments more than once—then stopping, unable
or unwilling to continue. As with the letter from my mother to my father
when he was in Spain, I have a memory—now over forty years old—of
finding notes toward the story about the woman my father called Marian,
the actual name of his friend Bender's wife. And like my mother's letter
written sometime in 1937, these notes and a tentative beginning, written
sometime in 1969 or 1970, are lost, if they ever existed at all. I cannot find
them. If they never existed, then I have made it all up, an unfinished story,
adding the details as I imagined or wished them to be.

CHAPTER 22

Some years ago I began a correspondence with a childhood friend and fellow "Communist child," a musician and music critic, Tom Manoff, a man who knows the Internet with the ease and familiarity that I know the streets and avenues of the Upper West Side of Manhattan where I have lived for over forty years. It all began with one photograph—my father, Maurine, my sister Emily, and me on the beach at Mohegan Lake where I spent many childhood summers. I must be about eleven or twelve, Emily eight or nine. My father lies back in the sun he worships, his body looking strong, his face at rest. Emily cuddles into Maurine's arms, and I am sitting next to them, staring at the lake, perhaps planning to dive in.

Soon more photos come to me, some on email, some preserved on Tommy's blog, where I can view them at will. My user name: Kishinev. My password: KishKish. And there are the old cobblestone streets with their muddy borders—it has rained, there is no drainage, or it is winter and the snow and ice melt along the sides of the not-quite-interlocking stones. There is the door to the old Jewish hospital—ancient ironwork, large round knobs, and, at least in the photograph on the Internet, the door is bright blue. Portraits of residents move past me with a click, as if I am turning the pages of an ancient photo album found in an attic or the back of a dusty closet. I don't know the people depicted, of course. Tom has found them by Googling residents of Kishinev in the early twentieth century, but they are familiar, their faces, their postures, their beings somehow unquestionably known. A "bagel vendor"—his beard and forelocks white, his face looking grim, the Russian cap seen on so many photographs of immigrants; his huge basket is filled with flatbread, more like Middle Eastern pita bread than the fat bagels we know; his ragged pants and loose boots leave no question of his poverty. A Roma couple in their draping scarves and loose clothes seated in front of a tent—she seems to be cooking in a large iron pot—"Gypsies." *We used to be afraid of the Gypsies who made their camps at the edge of the city*, I remember my father saying.

There is a map of the old city, and Tom has sent instructions on how to use it by inserting colors to identify important parts: pale pink for "Jew Street," green for the old Bazaar where I now think my father's family may have lived, blue for Asia Street, Armenia Street in purple, the ritual baths at the edge of the quarter, the river at the northeast of the city. There are several photographs of the old Jewish cemetery—its gate, its sprawling uneven design, close-ups of ancient tombstones that appear to be toppling or sliding out of the earth. These are the streets he walked as a child and young man.

◆◆

1921 or 1922, Kishinev, first Russia, before that Romania—then no longer even Kishinev, now Chisinău, Moldova, a small nation all its own. You and your family survived the years of the First World War, yet I recall no descriptions of what must have been a difficult time. Russian soldiers in retreat, savaging Jewish homes. German troops not far behind. But I have no memory of your telling us about this time. More stories lost, though talk of leaving must have begun then, thoughts becoming plans with each new letter from your sisters already in America.

You are saying good-bye to your home, the Jewish quarter, a large section in the eastern part of the city. It all fades behind you, then past you as the train moves west toward Antwerp, Belgium. I thought at first you boarded here, where the Red Star ocean liners dominate the docks, crowded with immigrants hoping to sail for America. But the ship manifest Tom found says you boarded in Cherbourg, France.

The suitcases you must have carried! Your parents' luggage, your own—all you had saved from the home you would never see again. I too had suitcases in my childhood—imaginary ones I carried now and then, but the image so powerful it was manifested physically: my aching, exhausted arms, the baggage of my anger, my conflicted love. Even now, past my seventieth year, the feeling comes at times at night or during a quiet evening. My arms begin to ache, sore, exhausted muscles, stretched skin, as if I have been carrying heavy suitcases too long.

I see you, nineteen years old, lugging those bags, perhaps parcels too, some slung over your shoulder, some strapped over your back as you make your way to the train.

><

It is autumn and mornings are dark again. I am into my sixth or seventh year of this writing. It is past six thirty and dawn has not yet broken through the night. I have let my dreams sink back into darkness too, desiring an oblivious peace more than their messages, repetitive images of strange hotels where I do and do not live—the white-walled empty rooms that are somehow at the same time filled with crowds. The emptiness is so vast I cannot contain it—it threatens the boundaries of my flesh. The crowds are so thick I can't breathe.

><

He has climbed the hills at the southern edge of the city, past the old cottages, past the Bac River and the bridge. He is surrounded by trees and shrubs—perhaps on a map it might look like dense forest. But here he is, and in this solitude he can see it all—past the small rural villages on the outskirts to the center where growing groups of comrades meet, talk, plan—anger turned to hope, despair to courage as they see themselves mirrored in each others' eyes. It will go on without him. He feels an emptiness inside he can hardly contain—an emptiness that at the same time is full of noise, people in his past, police, demonstrators, or anticipation of the future closing in. They will board the ship, if they are lucky, if they pass the medical examinations at the boarding. They will be shoved and pushed by the crowded mass of people he has read about in letters from his sisters, from family members of his neighbors. He can smell the smell of steerage, hard to breathe, crushed by bodies, yet alone. Tomorrow morning he will take his sister and his parents to the station. By this time in the afternoon he will be on the train.

He is looking out at his city—the Jewish quarter where he has lived all his life,

*the western sections where Christians live—and Turks—and Armenians—
even some wealthy Jews. He sees the church, the marketplace—he can make out
the colors, even from here. Too many emotions fill him, racing and clashing—
for all that has been done, for all that he will miss. Suddenly he has the image of
a garden, part inside—overgrown and densely hidden—part outside—damp
from rain.*

✦

On the SS Kroonland *once it left land behind and they hit the open sea, while
his parents slept in their tiny airless cabin, while his younger sister stared out
the porthole, standing on her toes to see the ocean she had never seen before, he
turned his back to the wall and read.*

    *On the bus to the factory in Philadelphia, where he wove cloth all day, and
on the trolley going home, he read Marx's* Capital *and Lenin's* What Is to
Be Done? *Later, through long nights in a small cell in the Philadelphia federal penitentiary, he read Dreiser and Sinclair Lewis, in later years attempted
Faulkner. In New York City, a single parent before that sometimes lonely and
difficult state was named, he read through long nights of a different sort—the
Russian classics again—*The Brothers Karamazov, *along with his daughter,
who was reading it for her high school English class, both of them amazed by
the depth of emotion, the vastness and variety of character and idea depicted in
one book. He read Dickens, enraptured by the stories, dismayed by the poverty
and cruelty, both familiar to him, yet enjoying, he had to admit, the unreal-
ity of everything always working out in the end.* The Mandarins, *by Simone
de Beauvoir, whose book about women he had discussed at length with his
daughter, and* Rebecca—*a best seller full of page-turning escape, but also a
haunting story about truth and lies, the way a lie, if bold enough, can become
the story everyone tells, remembers, is even changed by. He read children's books
to his daughters, then chapter books—*Big Susan, *a story about dolls coming
to sudden life on Christmas Eve—that enticing blurred line again between
reality and fantasy, ordinary life and dreams. Later,* Little Women, Call of
the Wild, *and* Johnny Got His Gun *by Dalton Trumbo, giving both girls
nightmares, a man with no legs or arms, no sight or hearing, his body deci-
mated by war, yet his humanity, his mind, preserved. Giving him nightmares
too—about his own work in Spain—all the killing he'd been part of, in charge
of at times. Then he would turn to the novels of Howard Fast to remind him*

of principle, history's demands and purposes, stories about his heroes—Tom Paine, Toussaint L'Ouverture—the reason for all the sacrifice and death.

Nightmares came. How could they not? The illness and hunger of the passengers in steerage. The families who remembered the pogrom of '05 when he was an infant, then a kid listening to stories. And these memories were easy compared to Spain, the losses, the young faces, boys not much younger than his daughters now, twenty, twenty-one, some he'd recruited who never returned—and young women too—the nurses he had known about—some of them innocent yet killed along with some of the doctors—traitors among them, yes, but the others—also killed. It was war, he often said, when his daughter, outraged and astonished by the alarming reality of good people doing horrifying things, shouted at him once about right and wrong—tears streaming down her cheeks—and he'd repeated time and time again, It was war, it was war—her voice—his voice. And the nightmares came, some recalled only as a sense of terror, sometimes an image of something he couldn't place, fading fast.

He was startled by the clarity of some of the other dreams—like watching a movie, he watched the stories unfold—at times a witness as well as a participant. In these dreams things worked out better than in life. The dolls actually did come alive and enact their family dramas on the night before Christmas. Beth March did not die but stood in the shadow between the old couch and green velvet chair his dead wife always sat in after a long workday, her feet in those silver and blue striped slippers tucked under her as she drank a scotch and soda to ease her transition from the office to home. He was saying Kkaddish after all, standing in the Philadelphia synagogue he and his brother had mocked, even to his father's face, but his mother stood by him, reminding him of the Hebrew words.

In the past few weeks he had tried to write a story about Marian, how she left him after her cancer diagnosis, refusing to tell him where she'd gone to live the last months of her life, but he could not complete the story, could not find the words to match his feelings, not in English, and what would be the point of writing in Yiddish or Russian, even if he could remember the nuanced words?

He returned to reading. He'd read through every evening when his daughters were asleep, and long into the night after they had grown up and moved out, leaving him with empty rooms, dusty furniture, darkening wood floors—though he did have the window cleaner in twice a year, and he did make his bed every morning, and he did change his sheets, freshly cleaned and

ironed into crisp folds at the Chinese laundry down the street, where he kib-
itzed with Won Gon Ju—never sharing the joke with the store owner, how
the man's name named them both—Won Gon Ju and one gone Jew. He was
alone, so to ease it all, he read—Shakespeare's tragedies, especially King Lear,
Carl Sandberg's multivolume biography of Abraham Lincoln, the New Left
theorists and the liberal commentators. The only two subjects he stayed away
from were the mea culpas by his old comrades who now wanted to denounce
everything in which they had once believed, and psychoanalysis, a subject he
left entirely to his daughter now that she was "in it" and studying it, and for all
he knew planning to become one.

Plenty to read. More than he could accomplish in a lifetime.

CHAPTER 23

It was a cold but clear December in the midst of a strike by telephone installation workers, so, recently moved into our New York apartment, we did not have a phone. Lois and Frederick lived nine floors up. Somehow, I had convinced the managing company executive to rent us two apartments in the same building, even though only one was officially advertised. Having recently migrated from North Carolina to New York City to be near their children and grandson, Douglas's parents had lived for months in one room in an old building on Upper Broadway. Now they enjoyed three rooms, a full kitchen, a terrace. When the bell rang and my father's coworker's voice came over the intercom—in the way that you know things you have hardly dared to imagine before—I knew my father was dead. I left Adam with his grandmother and rushed downtown.

Lorenzo had called Douglas at his office to say Bill had not been at work since the previous morning and had not called in. Since there was no way to reach me by phone, this kind man who had become my father's friend agreed to come uptown to bring me the news. Meanwhile Douglas raced to the Greenwich Avenue apartment to which he still had the key.

So he was the first to find my father. Then he called my Uncle Jack, brother of Ernest Arion who had died in Spain, and George Charney—old friends still the closest in an emergency. When I arrived, the three men stood between the living room and kitchen/dining room, making a grim triangle in the archway. Douglas embraced me. I moved quickly into my father's room.

His book lay opened on the night table. The television was on, but all he ever watched on a regular basis was the eleven o'clock news. It was the second of December, so we knew it must have been the first of December when he died. He was lying on the floor next to the opened closet, which had a small shelf attached to the door. Years before, my mother used to keep her crystal perfume bottles there, and for the past few years he'd kept his nitroglycerin tablets on the same shelf. The tablets were scattered on the floor next to his body. The bottle was clutched in his frozen hand.

Epilogue

Through the years of writing this memoir, I have experienced a change that is foundation and consequence at once: I now possess some fuller understanding of my father's life and the history he lived through. With that come both the pain of opportunities forever lost and the relief of understanding itself.

I remember his criticisms, of clothes, aspects of my personality, my emotional outbursts, and even of my body when during early adolescence I began to gain weight, especially in my stomach.

I remember those private words I whispered when my mother died: *Now I have to make daddy love me*, and how as the child of seven I was then—and for many years afterwards—I fully believed the truth of those words; and I remember his denial of their truth shortly before his death. But as I write toward the end of the story, I see another layer. I was seven, living in the center of powerful unconscious love. Perhaps later on I changed the words slightly and left one word out, a protection from the guilty pleasure that over years had to be "forgotten." Now I *can* make my daddy love me—*best*, I might have whispered in that long ago moment. Memory is notoriously self-serving, one truth can exist among others, a story within a story crafters of fiction know well. This idea itself may be true or only my latest distortion, but as I write, it comes to mind.

I remember sitting next to him on our living room couch gripped by the Army-McCarthy hearings, the relatively new and increasingly widespread technology of television revealing that long American disgrace to the world.

I am incurring his wrath, and worse, his disappointment in me, in my sense of dignity, when I am caught by Mr. Nash on the roof where I have been making out with my boyfriend, our rumpled clothes and the shared lipstick stains on our cheeks and lips making our shameful activities all too clear.

I am sitting in a chair in his room, facing him, an open book in my hands, reporting on my reading of the week. I am excited, fascinated, and a bit nervous as I enter into a discussion of a novel by Maxim Gorky or Howard Fast, a small excerpt by Marx or Lenin, a poem by Walt Whitman, usually "O Captain! My Captain!" or "The Road Not Taken" by Robert Frost.

Later in my college years, when I read about the fetishism of commodities and reported to my father who, in my opinion, did not fully appreciate the argument which had just opened a wide enticing place in my comprehension of all the social forces I had been asked to contemplate for years, I probably shouted—"Our obsession with commodities becomes a fetish! A fetish that extends to everything, the way we relate to each other, the way we understand knowledge itself!" I may have been swinging the slim red leather-covered volume in my hands in a wide dramatic arc as I spoke. "Do you see what that means Dad? Our very concepts of knowledge itself!?" I remember clearly that old transforming shift, even if not my exact words.

I am rereading his letters to me when I was in Italy, happily remembering his words of pride.

I am walking behind an eighteen-month-old Adam as he races down the hallway into my father's waiting arms.

I am watching silently as my forty-two-year-old son Khary reads a draft of this story about the grandfather he never knew yet who is so similar to him in some ways it can lead me to believe that the handing down of spirit is as material as the handing down of genes.

><

He valued respect for all people, for himself, for all of us—children of his blood and children of his heart, many of whom still tell me of his special claim to their love—an emotional openness they were unaccustomed to in their fathers. He got things wrong at times, of course he did—confusing self-respect with self-control and sexual abstinence, certainly for girls, and, worse perhaps, denying evidence of murderous policies, mass imprisonments and killings by Stalin until it was far too late to blame counterrevolutionaries, surrounding hostile nations, or the capitalist press. His denials and mistakes were in part—as they are for all of us—a fear of moving one step beyond what he knew for sure and needed to believe, a lack of awareness of some of the forces and realities we now think of as self-evident. He lived at the very beginning of a time when the dramatic new consciousness of second-wave feminism began to redefine the way we understand our sexuality and our sexual histories, the ways patriarchal structures have constrained all our lives, and women's voices, for centuries, and he died before those early insights were further developed by scholars and artists into a cultural awareness that can no longer easily be denied. His dedication to the Party was his foundation, his early faith only momentarily shaken, fully broken late, and then only when Soviet leaders themselves acknowledged what had been seen for years by disappointed progressives outside the world of dedicated Communists. We, his descendants and some of our comrades— still a good word, a very specific and evocative word—know things now he did not know, and we have been altered by this understanding. In the grip of such alterations comes the knowledge that while we all have a hand in creating our own stories, we are also embedded in and in some ways controlled by the cultures and assumptions of our time. Seeing through that embeddedness is possible, and we know this from history, some of us from personal experience. Not seeing through it is always a danger. The only way to address that danger is to assume the humility of knowing it exists.

Something within me moves to a different place—a new perspective as undeniable as a move from a front to a side view in a portrait by Picasso, or a storyteller's decision to suddenly shift time or point of view. Certain aspects of this shift are clear to me—how I remember my history as my father's daughter, what I understand of the broader history into which I was born and grew to adulthood, a history that for my father was never abstract or distant, rather always immediate, intimate, and personal. In all these changes, known and unknown, named or to be named in some future time, or never to be named at all, I have a different image of myself than when I first began receiving Tom's emails and gazed at the streets of old

Kishinev or read my father's name on the manifest of the ship that brought him to America.

❧

In Toni Morrison's novel *Home*, a character reminds herself of words she has heard from a maternal figure who has saved her life: "Look to yourself," she remembers the older woman saying. "You free. Nothing and nobody is obliged to save you but you. Seed your own land. You young and a woman and there's serious limitation in both, but you a person too. . . . Somewhere inside you is that free person I'm talking about. Locate her and let her do some good in the world."[1]

For an older person, even an old person, this advice holds true. The free person inside I was long ago, when I held onto what I believed even as those adults I loved and trusted denied the truth and concocted their own lies, that capacity that developed in part as a resistance to my father, is part of my history. But so is the history of Bill Lazarre and many of his comrades who never gave up fighting the good fight—as some of their descendants continue to do, believing that we are all connected in powerful ways even as racism and economic injustice divide us. I know as a mother that those who have begun life inside my body are never entirely *outside* of me again, and that reality can also be a metaphor for attachment to many others. An idealistic notion—but without ideals, reality can be narrow and dull. We are wise to protect ourselves with boundaries from threats of many kinds; and we are better and saner for recognizing the need for keeping those boundaries flexible and fluid, strengthening the human capacity for what Virginia Woolf, through the artist Lily Briscoe, called "intimacy itself." This is as true in collective as in personal life.

I believe my father somehow possessed both strengths in his fight against tyranny, that he knew something of the unity of the two freedoms we once fought over as unbridgeable contradictions. Somehow he communicated this unity, or I doubt I would have pursued it in the same way throughout my own life. The old country of Kishinev and the old country of the psyche have always been joined. If I think of "resistance" in its psychological meaning as a form of self-protection against forces ranged against one's safety and integrity, and add to it the many historical instances of collective and individual resistance to political tyranny, then writing has always been, outside and inside, a beautiful resistance.

⤚⤙

It was a cold winter afternoon the last time I saw him alive. He was walking me to the 12th Street subway station where I would head uptown to my new home, leaving him in the one we'd shared over so many different times. As I embraced him, he felt my cold hands. He took off his blue woolen gloves and insisted I put them on, shoved his own hands into the deep pockets of the navy blue pea jacket he always wore. Suffused with a feeling of parting again, infused in a new way with his being, I end with a few of my father's own words—part of a letter left to my sister and me to be read after his death.

> To me the pains, sufferings and hardships of the multitude were my pains and hardships. I profoundly believe in the righteousness of the cause I worked for and still do. The fact that I would do things differently in my latter years does not negate the justice of the idea I hoped to realize in my lifetime. Independent thought and action does not contradict sensitive response to the feelings of others. I am proud of many things I have taken part in which the American people today take for granted. My work in Spain is one of my greatest prides. My rich years were more than seven and overshadowed the lean ones. I lived as I chose to live. As I wanted to live.

ACKNOWLEDGMENTS

Epigraph: Sebastian Barry, *The Temporary Gentleman* (New York: Viking, 2014);
© 2014 Sebastian Barry. Muriel Rukeyser, "Orpheus," in *Selected Poems*, edited by
Adrienne Rich (Boone, IA: Library of America, 2004); © 2004 William Rukeyser.

PROLOGUE

Epigraph: Toni Morrison, "The Site of Memory," in *Inventing the Truth: The Art and
Craft of Memoir*, edited by William Zinsser (New York: Houghton Mifflin, 1995);
© Toni Morrison.
  1 The Brotherhood-Sister Sol, an organization serving the needs of children and
    youth in New York City.
  2 Jane Lazarre, "Forgiveness," a story in the *Village Voice*, May 19, 1975.

CHAPTER 1

Epigraph: Patricia Hampl, *I Could Tell You Stories: Sojourns in the Land of Memory*
(New York: W. W. Norton, 1999); © 1999 Patricia Hampl.

CHAPTER 3

Epigraph: Langston Hughes, "I, Too, Sing America," in *The Collected Poems of
Langston Hughes* (New York: Alfred A. Knopf, 1994). © 1994 Estate of Langston
Hughes.

CHAPTER 4

Epigraph: Words of the sitting judge of the Superior Court of Pennsylvania, Eastern District, in the "Appeal from the Judgment and Sentence of the Court of Quarter Sessions of the County of Philadelphia," April Sessions 1929, no. 44, *Commonwealth v. Israel Lazar*, appellant. All quotations and excerpts from the appeal in Philadelphia are from *The Judgment and Sentence of the Court of Quarter Sessions of the County of Pennsylvania*, April Sessions 1929, no. 44, *Commonwealth v Israel Lazar*, appellant. All spellings have been kept as in document. Final reference to appeal joined by American Civil Liberties Union in *Sweet Land of Liberty, 1931–1932* (New York: American Civil Liberties Union, 1932); pages 9 and 13 pertain to "Pardon Application for Israel Lazar, also known as Bill Lawrence, sentenced to two to four years under The Pennsylvania Sedition Act."

  1 Lèse-majesté is a law offending the dignity of a sovereign or speaking against the state.
  2 George Charney, *A Long Journey* (Chicago: Quadrangle Books, 1968).

CHAPTER 5

Epigraph: Frederick Douglass, *The Life and Times of Frederick Douglass: From 1817–1882* (Boston: De Wolfe & Fiske, 1892). Quoted as an epigraph by Natasha Trethewey in *Native Guard*, a poem made from the journals of African American soldiers in the Civil War.

  1 Bill Lawrence, "Farewell to Americans in Spain," in the *Volunteer*, then called the *Volunteer for Liberty*, October 25, 1937.
  2 Earl Browder, with Bill Lawrence, *Next Steps to Win the War in Spain* (New York: Worker's Library, 1938); Bill Lawrence, *Democracy's Stake in Spain* (New York: Worker's Library, 1938), both passim.

CHAPTER 7

  1 Edwin Rolfe, *The Lincoln Battalion: The Story of the Americans Who Fought in Spain in the International Brigades* (New York: Random House, 1939), chapter 1, "Those Who Fought," 5–57.
  2 Peter N. Carroll, *The Odyssey of the American Lincoln Brigade: Americans in the Spanish Civil War* (Stanford, California: Stanford University Press, 1994), 9.
  3 Carroll, *Odyssey of the American Lincoln Brigade*, 99, 100.
  4 Helen Graham, *The Spanish Civil War: A Very Short Introduction* (Oxford: Oxford University Press, 2005), 161.
  5 Graham, *Spanish Civil War*, 2, 6.
  6 Graham, *Spanish Civil War*, 2, 5–9 passim.
  7 Carroll, *Odyssey of the American Lincoln Brigade*; Graham, *Spanish Civil War*.
  8 Bill Lawrence, *Democracy's Stake in Spain* (New York: Worker's Library, 1938), passim.
  9 Carroll, *Odyssey of the American Lincoln Brigade*, 376.
  10 Quoted from interview with John Murra by John Doyle. Contained in Murra's pa-

pers, available online and at Tamiment Library at New York University, Archives of Abraham Lincoln Brigade, http://www.nyu.edu/library/bobst/research/tam /index.html, posted June 1, 2010.

11 Carroll, *Odyssey of the American Lincoln Brigade*, 163.

12 Adam Hochschild, *Spain in Our Hearts: Americans in the Spanish Civil War, 1936–1939* (New York: Houghton Mifflin Harcourt, 2016).

13 Rolfe, *Lincoln Battalion*, 17, 88.

CHAPTER 9

1 Giles Tremlett, *Ghosts of Spain: Travels through Spain and Its Silent Past* (New York: Bloomsbury, 2006), 9, 10.

2 George Charney, *A Long Journey* (Chicago: Quadrangle Books, 1968), 277–79 passim.

3 Peter N. Carroll, *The Odyssey of the American Lincoln Brigade: Americans in the Spanish Civil War* (Stanford, California: Stanford University Press, 1994), 202–3.

CHAPTER 10

Epigraph: Adrienne Rich, poem *XVII* of "Twenty-One Love Poems," in *The Dream of a Common Language: Poems 1974–1977* (New York: W. W. Norton, 1978).

1 Alan Furst, *Dark Star* (New York: Random House, 1991), 193.

2 George Charney, *A Long Journey* (Chicago: Quadrangle Books, 1968), 133.

3 Peter N. Carroll, *The Odyssey of the American Lincoln Brigade: Americans in the Spanish Civil War* (Stanford, CA: Stanford University Press, 1994), 277, 278.

4 Jacques Duclos, "On the Dissolution of the Communist Party of the United States," Published in *Cahiers du Communisme*, April 1945.

5 Charney, *Long Journey*, 141–44 passim.

6 Charney, *Long Journey*, 140.

CHAPTER 11

1 George Charney, *A Long Journey* (Chicago: Quadrangle Books, 1968), 140.

CHAPTER 13

All references to and quotes from Federal Bureau of Investigation interviews and memos are from the Freedom of Information and Privacy Acts, US Department of Justice, sections 1–6.

CHAPTER 16

Epigraphs: James Baldwin, "Notes of a Native Son" in *Notes of a Native Son* (Boston, Beacon Press, 1975), 113; Joint Resignation Statement by George Charney, William Lawrence, George Watt, April 1958, in *Party Voice* (the written organ of the New York State Communist Party).

1 From FBI file, 1951–1958.

CHAPTER 17

1 Testimony of William Lazar before the House Committee on Un-American Activities, June 1958, New York City, https://archive.org/stream/communism innewyooounit/communisminnewyooounit_djvu.txt.
2 "Testimony of Paul Robeson before the House Committee on Un-American Activities, June 12, 1956," History Matters, historymatters.gmu.edu/d/6440.

CHAPTER 18

1 Maurice Isserman, *Which Side Are You On?* (Urbana: University of Illinois Press, 1993), 250.
2 George Charney, *A Long Journey* (Chicago: Quadrangle Books, 1968), 257.
3 Charney *A Long Journey,* 323.

CHAPTER 19

Epigraph: Adam Zagajewski, "Try to Praise the Mutilated World," in *Without End: New and Selected Poems*, translated from the Polish by Clare Cavanaugh (New York: Farrar, Strauss and Giroux, 2002). Translation copyright © 2002 Farrar, Strauss and Giroux.

1 Reading through some of Bukharin's letters on the Internet, compiled by various authors, and his autobiographical novel, *How It All Began*, I assume my father probably read through some of this material as well. Actual quotations from Bukharin are taken from excerpts from his letters, including his last letter to Stalin, written from prison before his execution.

CHAPTER 21

Epigraph: Eugene Mahon, *All Serious Daring* (New York: Deluge Books, 2011).

EPILOGUE

1 Toni Morrison, *Home* (New York: Alfred A. Knopf, 2012), 126.